CONTENTS

INTRODUCTION

"My students really enjoy working at independent learning centers!"

"Learning centers are colorful, attractive, and add interest to the curriculum!"

"Manipulatives are helping me break out of the worksheet habit!"

Teachers all over are rediscovering the benefits of learning centers, which can challenge advanced students, as well as help slower students brush up weak skill areas. But some teachers are worried that learning centers take a lot of time to create, or that artistic skills are required to make the centers appealing.

That's where this book comes in. *Stories & Songs* provides all the patterns and activities you need to construct ten self-contained math skills learning centers. Each of the centers features five different activities that focus on a particular skill, enabling the center to be used in a variety of ways. Activities are provided both for individual work and for cooperative learning. And you can decide whether to have children complete one activity a day, or work through an entire center at their own speed.

All the centers in *Stories & Songs* are literature based, so you can incorporate them into larger units of study. The story and song themes, such as "Jack and the Beanstalk" and "I've Been Working on the Railroad," are favorites with children, and can be used to stimulate reading, creative writing, drama, art, even playground fun. Each center has a suggested grade level indicated, but choose the skills you want to work on according to the needs of your students.

While the centers can be used in a number of ways, they're easy to construct and don't require artistic talent or hard-to-find materials. Each center provides directions for arranging and working with the materials for each activity, and directions for constructing the learning center display panels are given here.

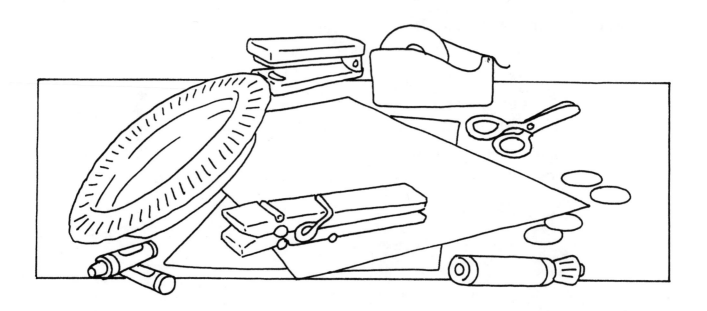

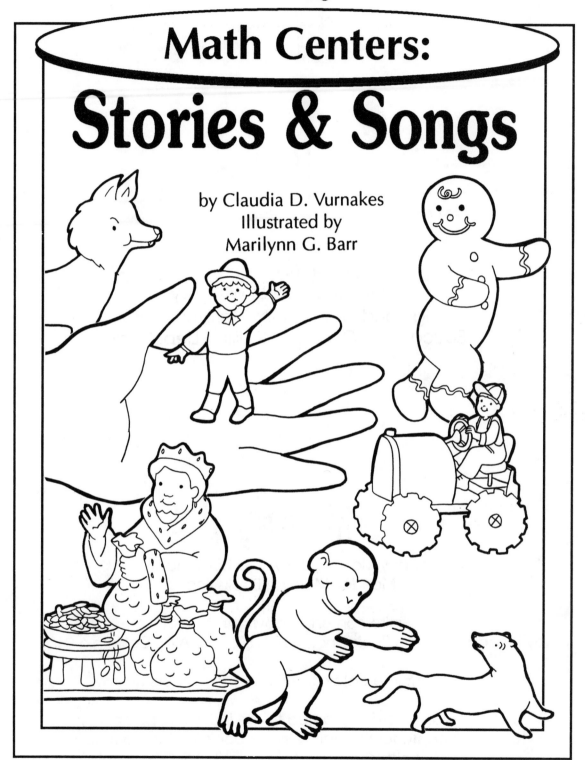

Math Centers:
Stories & Songs

by Claudia D. Vurnakes
Illustrated by
Marilynn G. Barr

Publisher: Roberta Suid
Copy Editor: Carol Whiteley
Design and Production: Marilynn G. Barr
Educational Consultant: Lillian Lieberman

Monday Morning Books is a trademark of
Monday Morning Books, Inc.

ISBN 1-878279-58-0

Printed in the United States of America

9 8 7 6 5 4 3 2 1

CONSTRUCTING THE LEARNING CENTERS

The learning centers described here are free-standing, folded panels. We recommend using three panels per center that measure approximately 19" x 24" each, but feel free to alter the dimensions to suit your classroom space and storage area.

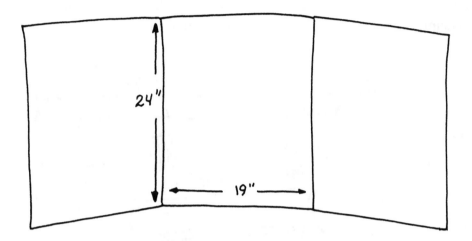

Use a stiff, strong material for your learning center panels—both corrugated cardboard and foam art board work well. You may want to glue bright paper to the panels or spray-paint them to provide colorful, eye-catching backgrounds. Small art pieces are provided in each chapter that you can color and glue to the panels for additional appeal.

Hinge the panels together with durable tape at least two inches wide; duct tape is great for this. Position the panels so that you have a quarter- to a half-inch gap between them. Then tape the fronts and backs to make hinges that will allow you to fold the panels flat for storage. You may also want to tape the outside edges of the center to prevent frayed corners. The time you spend constructing a durable center will really pay off.

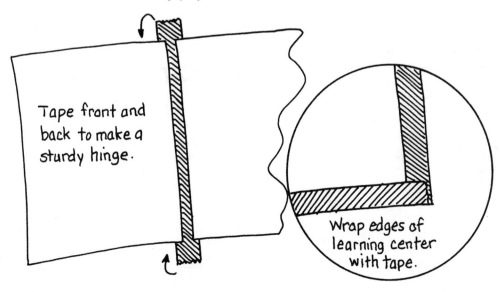

Tape front and back to make a sturdy hinge.

Wrap edges of learning center with tape.

ADDING SKILL PROGRAMMING

Duplicate the pages from this book for the learning center you want to make. Use markers, paint, or crayons to add color. Then cut out and glue the activities in position on your panels, using the illustration of the completed learning center at the front of the chapter as a guide.

For durable activity pieces and game boards, mount the pages on poster board and laminate before cutting them out. If you want to code the backs of pieces for self-checking, be sure to do that before you laminate.

STORING CENTER MATERIALS

Most of the activities are manipulative, so you need to plan how you will store the materials. For pockets glued or stapled directly on the panels, use paper plates cut in half, small flat boxes, manila envelopes, or library pocket cards. Some centers suggest other means of storing pieces, such as paper cups attached with clothespins to the center.

ADDITIONAL MATERIALS

All of the materials necessary, in addition to those duplicated from the book, are easy to obtain, such as paper clips, game markers, and pennies. A specific list of required materials is provided on the first page of each learning center chapter.

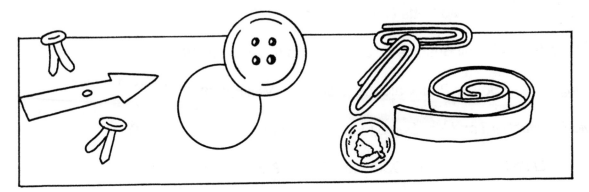

ADAPTING THE CENTERS TO OTHER SKILLS OR LEVELS

Many of the activities featured in *Stories & Songs* can be easily adapted to other grade levels or used for different skills entirely. Just substitute your own student instruction boxes for the ones given here. Reprogram game cards and word wheels for the desired skill. You can extend the life of a learning center by clipping new instructions over old ones.

RESOURCE LIST

STORIES:

Gingerbread Boy by David Cutts (Troll Associates, 1979).

Jack & the Beanstalk by Beatrice S. De Regniers (Macmillan, 1990).

The Gingerbread Boy by Paul Galdone (Houghton Mifflin, 1983).

Old Mother Hubbard and Her Dog by Paul Galdone (McGraw-Hill, 1961).

The Three Little Kittens by Paul Galdone (Ticknor & Fields, 1988).

Tom Thumb by the Brothers Grimm, translated by Anthea Bell (Larousse, 1976).

The Comic Adventures of Old Mother Hubbard and Her Dog by Catherine Martin (Harcourt, 1981).

Favorite Fairy Tales, edited by Jennifer Mulherin (Putnam, 1983).

Favorite Fairy Tales by Tasha Tudor (Putnam, 1990).

SONGS:

Mother Goose Melodies by E.F. Bleiler (Dover, 1985).

Mother Goose Songbook by Tom Glazer (Doubleday, 1990).

Tom Glazer's Treasury of Songs for Children by Tom Glazer (Doubleday, 1988).

A Collection of Favorite Children's Songs, edited by Jane Hart (Lothrop, 1989).

Songs from Mother Goose: With the Traditional Melody for Each, edited by Nancy Larrick (HarperCollins, 1989).

Three Little Pigs

Materials:
Storage pockets, paper cup,
clothespin, magnetic tape, paper clips,
poster board, wipe-off crayons,
glue, two-inch brad.

Three Little Pigs

1. _____
2. _____
3. _____
4. _____
5. _____

Before
After
After
Before
Before
After

1		3	4		6
	8			11	
13		15	16		18
		20			

2

5   7

8

4

3   5

1		
9	6	
17		
21	18	15
25	26	23
30		
		32

Number Sequence

Three Little Pigs

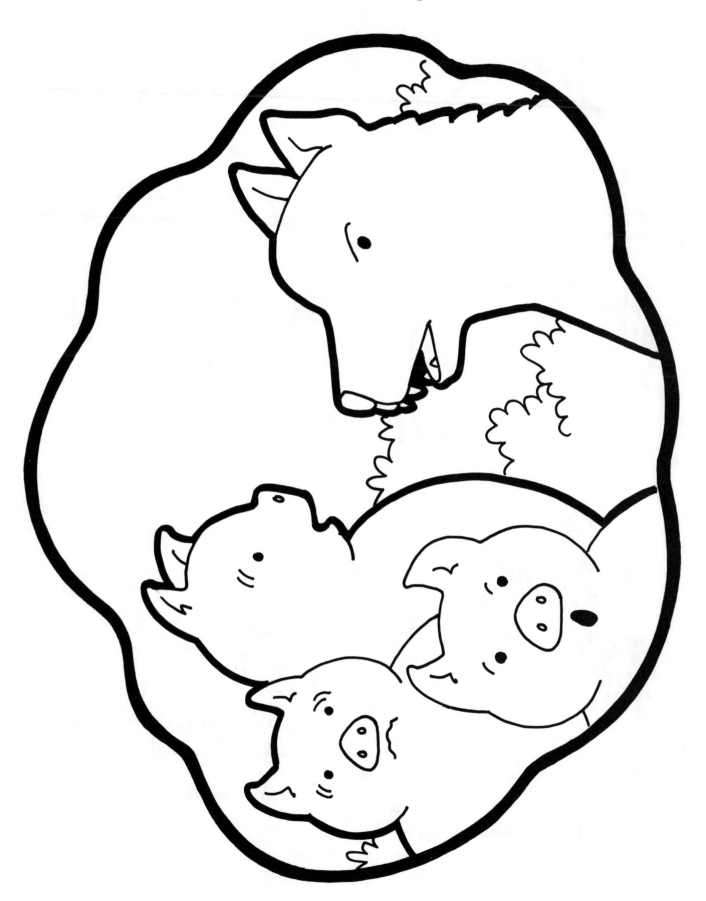

© 1993 Monday Morning Books, Inc.

Three Little Pigs

Three Little Pigs

1. For each twig house, find the missing number. Put it in the empty box.

Note: Use with number cards (page 20). Store house cards in pocket on center. Store number cards in cup clipped to center

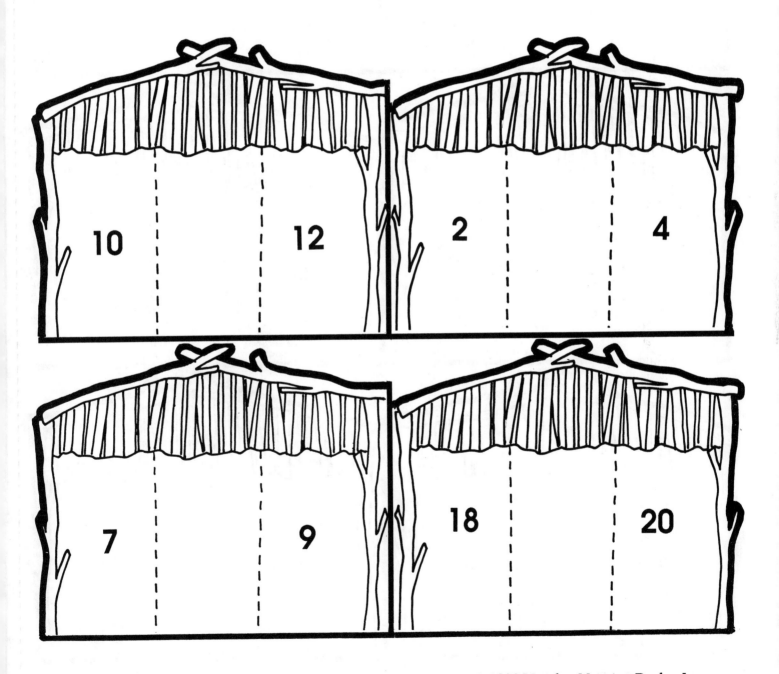

13

Three Little Pigs

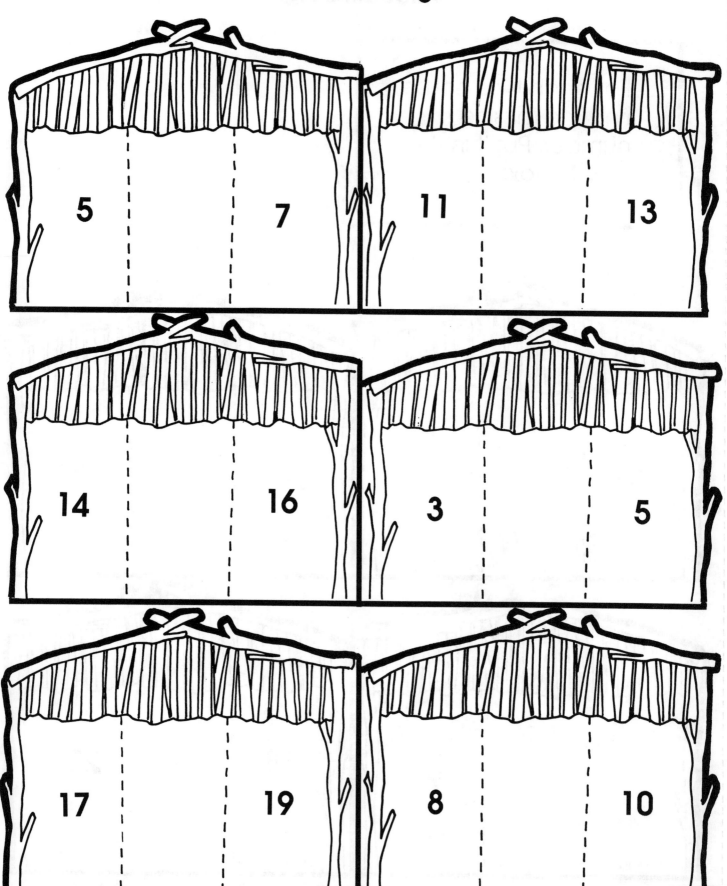

5   7   11   13

14   16   3   5

17   19   8   10

Stories & Songs

Three Little Pigs

2. Finish this house of straw. Put each number in the right place.

Note: Use with straw house card (page 16) and number cards (page 20). Store house card in pocket on center. Store number cards in cup clipped to center.

3. Use a wipe-off crayon. Write the missing numbers on the cooking pot.

Note: Use with cooking pot (page 17). Provide a wipe-off crayon.

Three Little Pigs

What comes before and after?

■　　6　　■　　　■　　8　　■

■　　11　　■　　　■　　17　　■

■　　9　　■　　　■　　5　　■

■　　15　　■　　　■　　13　　■

■　　18　　■　　　■　　10　　■

Three Little Pigs

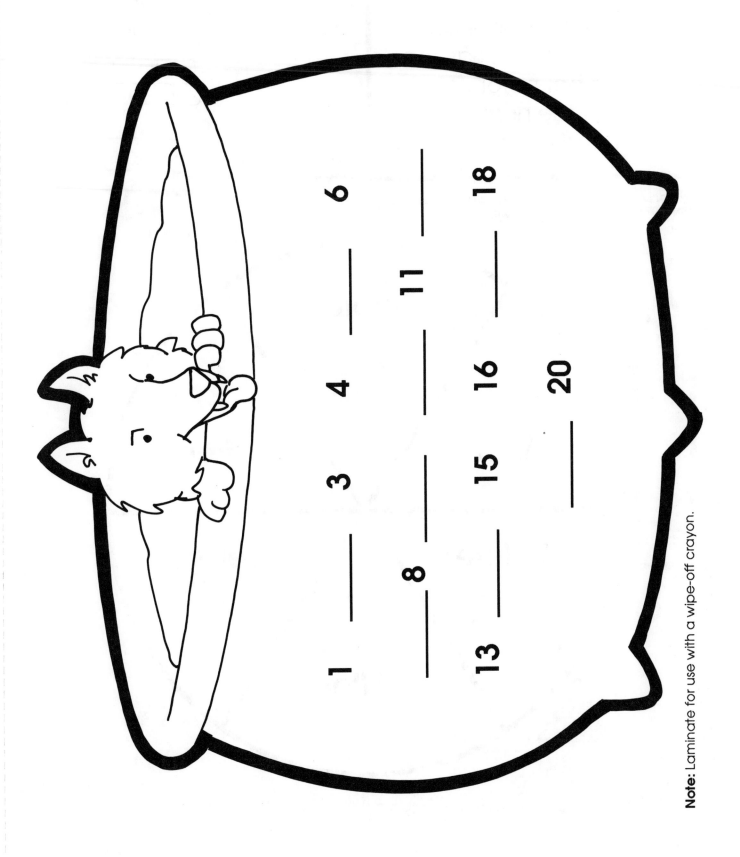

Three Little Pigs

4. Take a number card. Spin the dial. Say the number before or after the number on the card.

Note: Use with number cards (page 20). Store cards in pocket on center.

Note: Mount arrow on poster board and attach to wheel and center with two-inch brad.

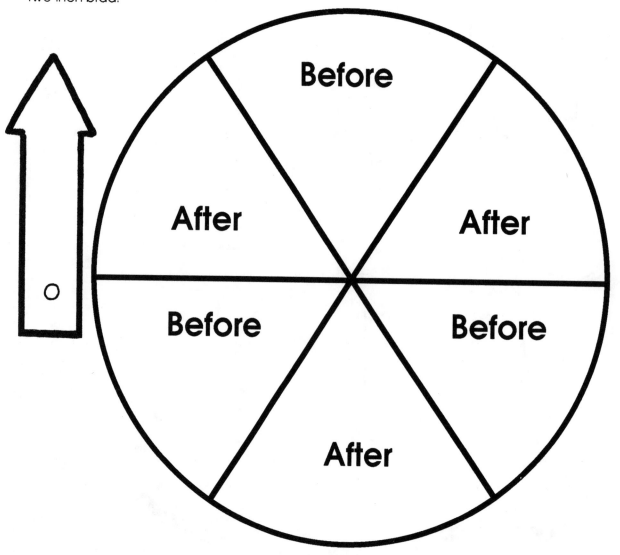

Three Little Pigs

5. Build a strong brick house! Write in missing numbers on the brick house cards.

Note: Laminate house cards and provide a wipe-off crayon. Store in pocket on center.

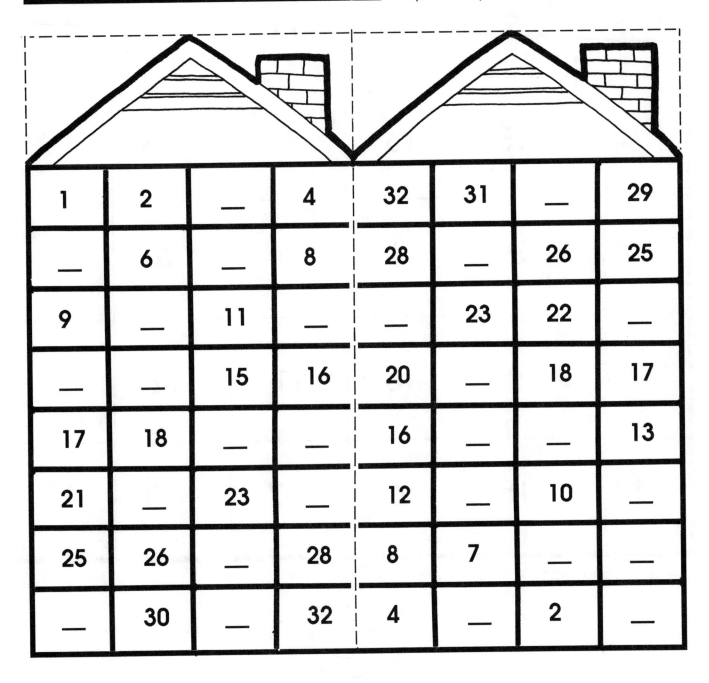

1	2	—	4	32	31	—	29
—	6	—	8	28	—	26	25
9	—	11	—	—	23	22	—
—	—	15	16	20	—	18	17
17	18	—	—	16	—	—	13
21	—	23	—	12	—	10	—
25	26	—	28	8	7	—	—
—	30	—	32	4	—	2	—

Three Little Pigs

2	3	4	5	6	7
8	9	10	11	12	13
14	15	16	17	18	19
2	3	4	5	6	7
8	9	10	11	12	13
14	15	16	17	18	19

Note: Number cards for Activities 1, 2, and 4.

20

Row, Row, Row Your Boat

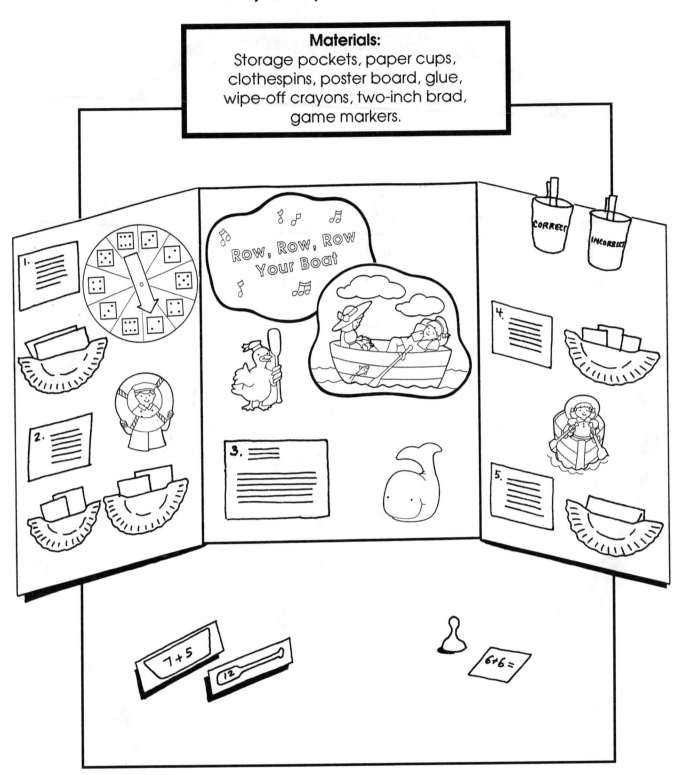

Materials:
Storage pockets, paper cups,
clothespins, poster board, glue,
wipe-off crayons, two-inch brad,
game markers.

Addition 1–12

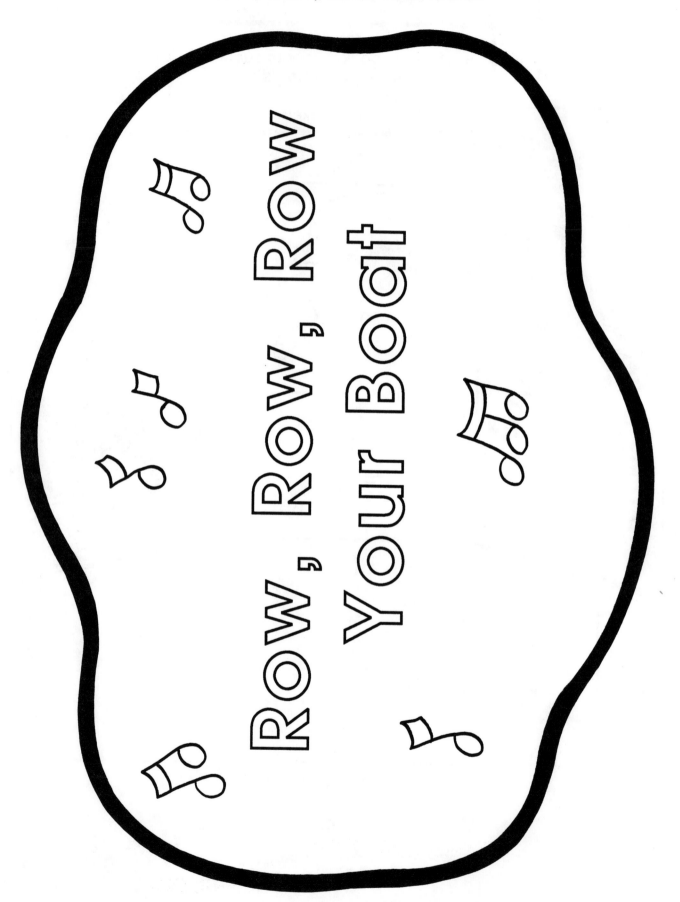

Stories & Songs

Row, Row, Row Your Boat

Row, Row, Row Your Boat

Row, Row, Row Your Boat

1. Take a problem sheet from the pocket. Spin the dial two times. Draw the dots in the first two empty squares and work the problem. Spin and work four more different problems.

Note: Duplicate problem sheet. Store copies in pocket on center.

□ + □ = ___ 7

□ + □ = ___

□ + □ = ___

□ + □ = ___

□ + □ = ___

□ + □ = ___

Row, Row, Row Your Boat

Note: Mount arrow on poster board and attach to wheel and center with two-inch brad.

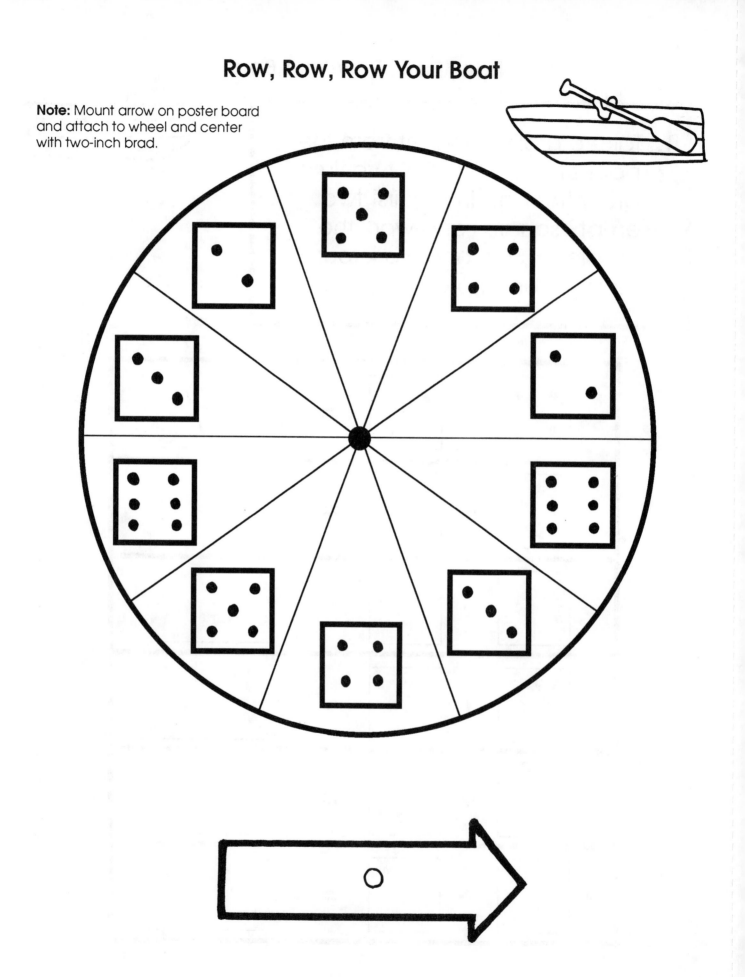

Row, Row, Row Your Boat

2. Match the boat and oar cards. Flip the boats over to check.

Note: Store cards in pockets on center.

Note: Write the correct sum on the back of each boat card.

6 + 6 =	12
6 + 3 =	9
6 + 4 =	10
7 + 3 =	10
7 + 4 =	11

Row, Row, Row, Your Boat

7 + 5 =	12
7 + 2 =	9
9 + 2 =	11
9 + 3 =	12
8 + 4 =	12
8 + 3 =	11
8 + 2 =	10

28   Stories & Songs

Row, Row, Row Your Boat

3. Use a wipe-off crayon to answer each problem. Use the letters to fill in the blanks at the bottom.

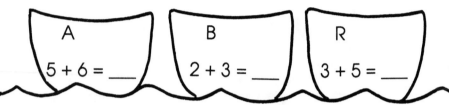

A   5 + 6 = ___   B   2 + 3 = ___   R   3 + 5 = ___

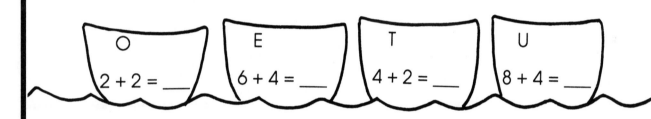

O   2 + 2 = ___   E   6 + 4 = ___   T   4 + 2 = ___   U   8 + 4 = ___

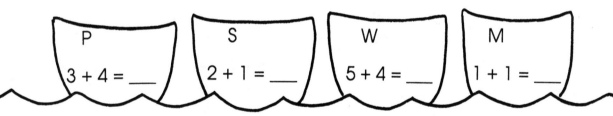

P   3 + 4 = ___   S   2 + 1 = ___   W   5 + 4 = ___   M   1 + 1 = ___

$\overline{8}\ \overline{4}\ \overline{9}\ \overline{5}\ \overline{4}\ \overline{11}\ \overline{6}\ \overline{3} \qquad \overline{12}\ \overline{3}\ \overline{10} \qquad \overline{11}\ \overline{8}\ \overline{2} \qquad \overline{7}\ \overline{4}\ \overline{9}\ \overline{10}\ \overline{8}\ !$

Note: Laminate and provide a wipe-off crayon.

Row, Row, Row Your Boat

4. Place each fact card in the right cup. Flip cards over to check.

Note: Clip cups to center with clothespins. Store cards in pocket.

Labels for paper cup buckets:

Correct

Incorrect

Cut out 32 game cards and label with the math facts here. Code the backs "I" or "C" for self-checking.

I		C
2 + 3 = 6	7 + 3 = 10	6 + 6 = 12
6 + 6 = 13	6 + 4 = 10	5 + 4 = 9
4 + 6 = 11	5 + 7 = 12	4 + 5 = 9
8 + 4 = 10	4 + 7 = 11	9 + 2 = 11
5 + 4 = 8	7 + 4 = 11	6 + 5 = 11
5 + 6 = 12	6 + 3 = 9	5 + 6 = 11
7 + 3 = 9	8 + 4 = 12	4 + 6 = 10
9 + 2 = 12	4 + 8 = 12	8 + 3 = 11
7 + 6 = 12	7 + 5 = 12	
7 + 4 = 10	5 + 3 = 8	
4 + 3 = 8	8 + 2 = 10	
5 + 3 = 9	9 + 3 = 12	

Row, Row, Row Your Boat

5. Game for Two Players

1. Put the game board on a table. In turn, draw a fact card.
2. Give the answer. The other player checks the answer key.
3. If correct, move ahead one space. If incorrect, stay where you are.
4. First to finish wins!

Answer Key

1. 12		11. 11	
2. 11		12. 10	
3. 11		13. 10	
4. 9		14. 8	
5. 10		15. 7	
6. 7		16. 9	
7. 8		17. 9	
8. 12		18. 11	
9. 8		19. 12	
10. 10		20. 12	

Note: Provide game markers. Store game board, answer key, and cards in pocket.

1. $9 + 3 =$ ___	2. $6 + 5 =$ ___	3. $8 + 3 =$ ___	4. $5 + 4 =$ ___
5. $7 + 3 =$ ___	6. $5 + 2 =$ ___	7. $6 + 2 =$ ___	8. $7 + 5 =$ ___
9. $4 + 4 =$ ___	10. $6 + 4 =$ ___	11. $9 + 2 =$ ___	12. $5 + 5 =$ ___
13. $8 + 2 =$ ___	14. $3 + 5 =$ ___	15. $4 + 3 =$ ___	16. $6 + 3 =$ ___
17. $7 + 2 =$ ___	18. $7 + 4 =$ ___	19. $6 + 6 =$ ___	20. $8 + 4 =$ ___

Row, Row, Row, Your Boat

32

Hickory Dickory Dock

Materials:
Storage pockets, poster board, glue,
two-inch brad, hole punch, string,
crayons, student paper.

Hickory Dickory Dock

1.

2.

3.

4.

5.

7:00

5:00

11:30

2:30

9:00

7:30

6:30

Time

33

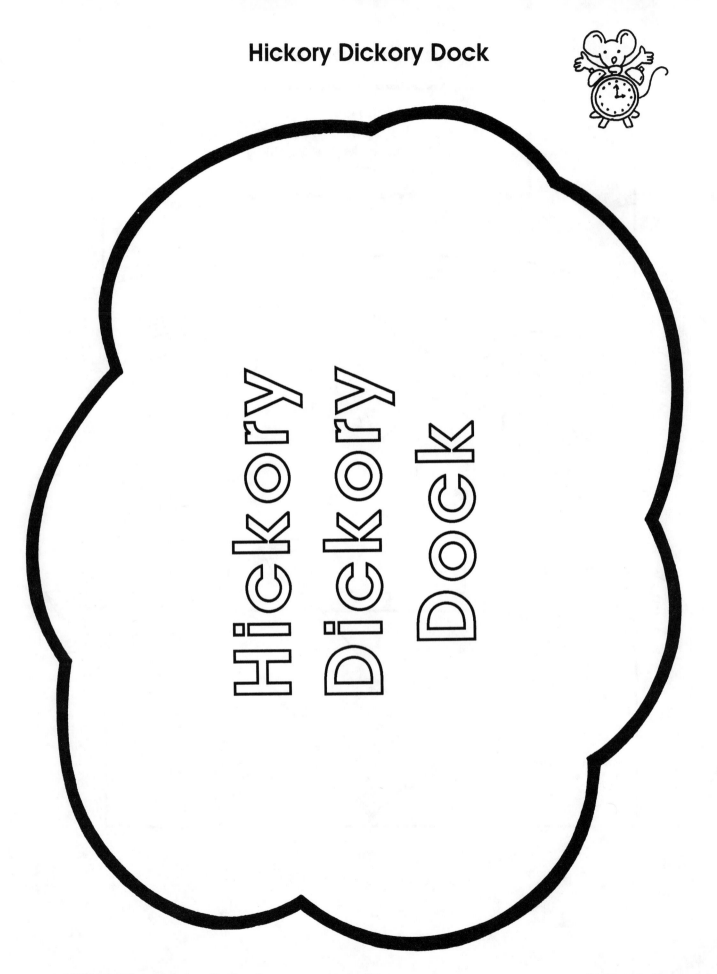

Hickory Dickory Dock

Hickory Dickory Dock

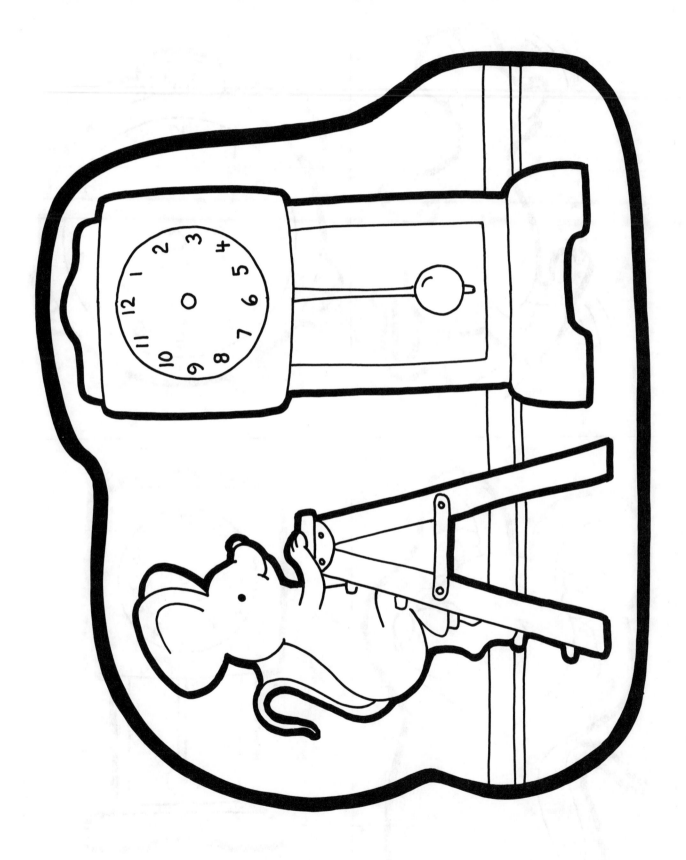

Hickory Dickory Dock

36

Hickory Dickory Dock

1. For each card in the pocket, show the correct time on the clock.

Note: Store cards in pocket on center.

Hickory Dickory Dock

Note: Mount clock hands on poster board. Attach to clock and center with two-inch brad.

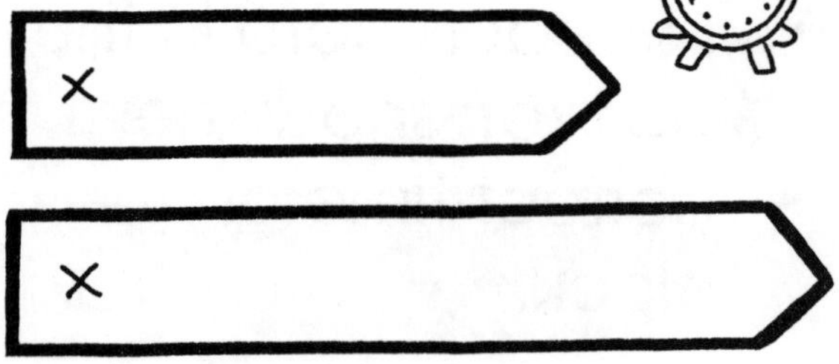

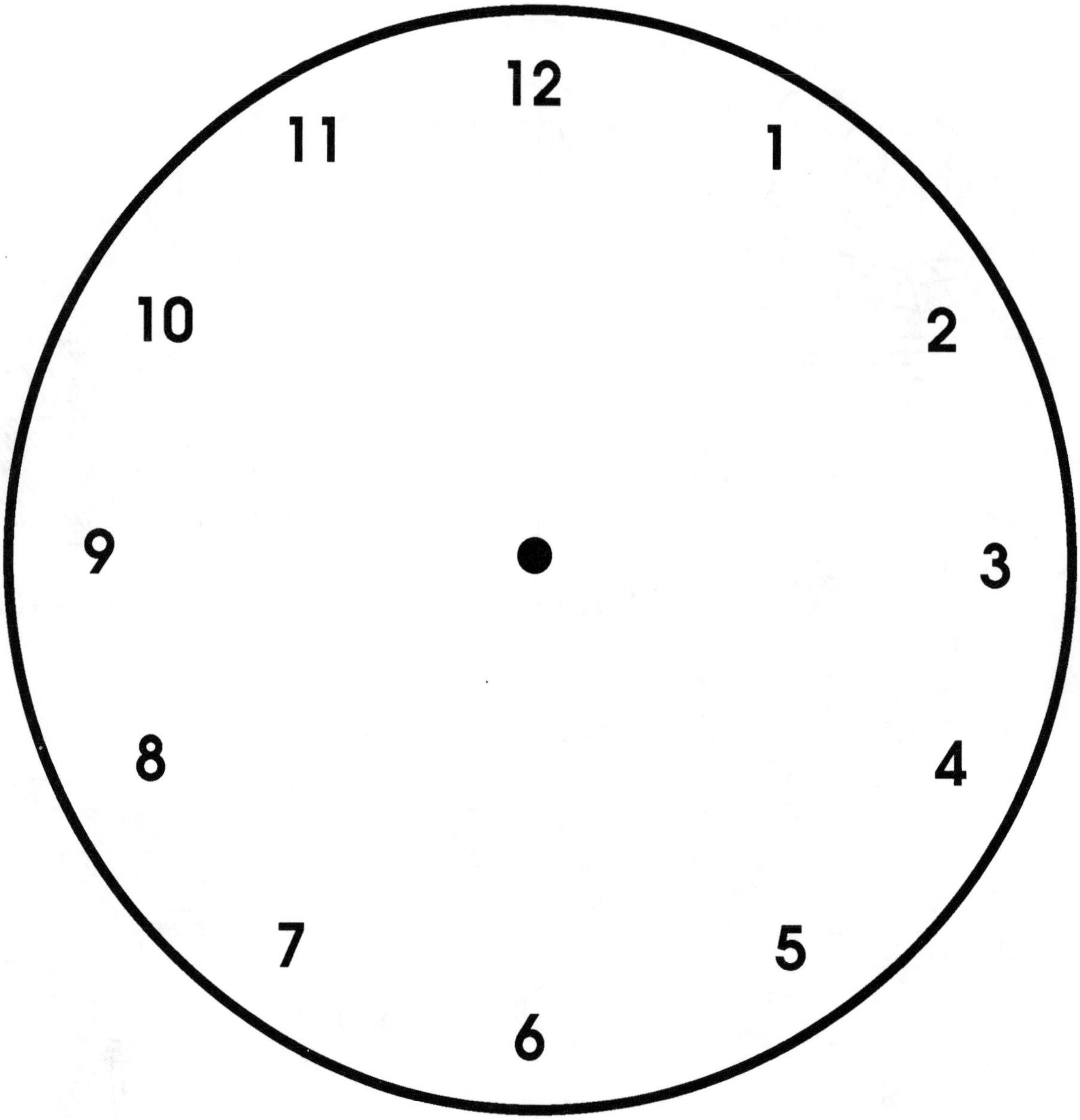

12

11

1

10

2

9

3

8

4

7

5

6

Hickory Dickory Dock

2. Match the clock cards and the time cards. Flip clock cards over to check.

Note: Store cards in pocket on center. Write correct time on backs of clock cards for self-checking.

(clock)	**1:30**	(clock)	**12:30**
(clock)	**3:30**	(clock)	**9:30**
(clock)	**7:30**	(clock)	**2:30**
(clock)	**2:00**	(clock)	**3:00**
(clock)	**4:30**	(clock)	**5:00**
(clock)	**6:30**	(clock)	**8:00**

Hickory Dickory Dock

3. Punch a hole by the clock that matches the time.

Note: Use string to tie hole punch to learning center. The activity may also be completed by coloring in the correct circles.

Duplicate number cards and store in pocket on center.

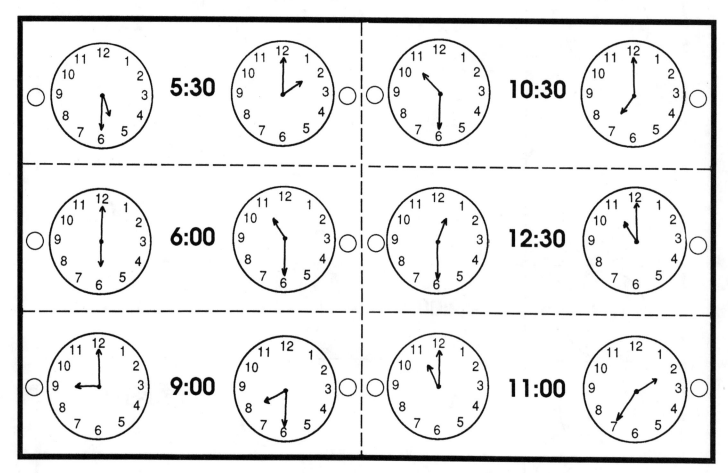

Hickory Dickory Dock

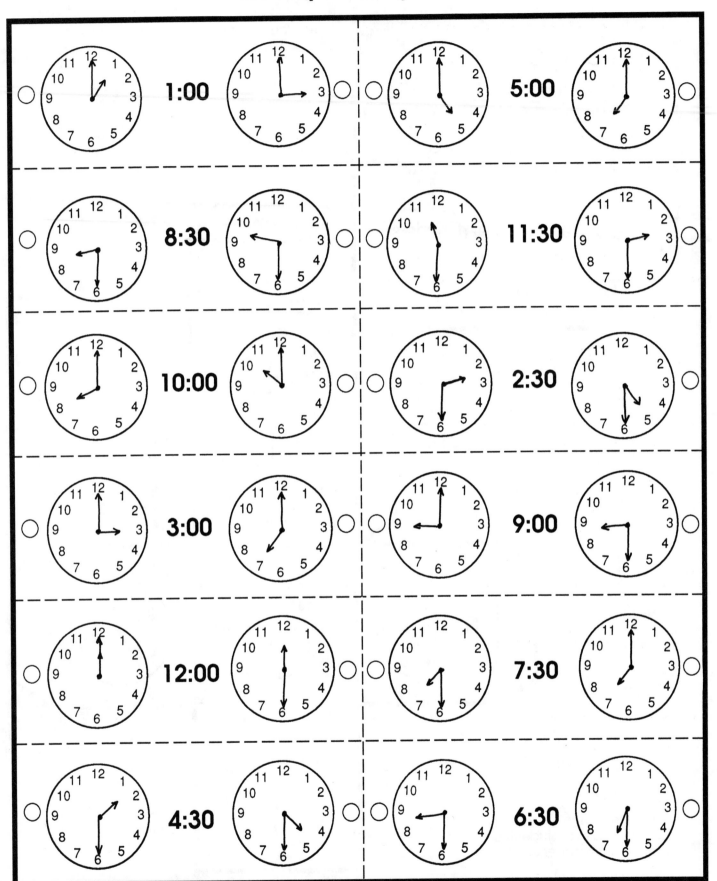

Hickory Dickory Dock

4. Roll-a-Clock! Roll the cube. On a piece of paper, write the time and draw a picture of what you do at that time. Roll for six different times and make six drawings.

Note: Mount on poster board, laminate front, and glue to form a cube.

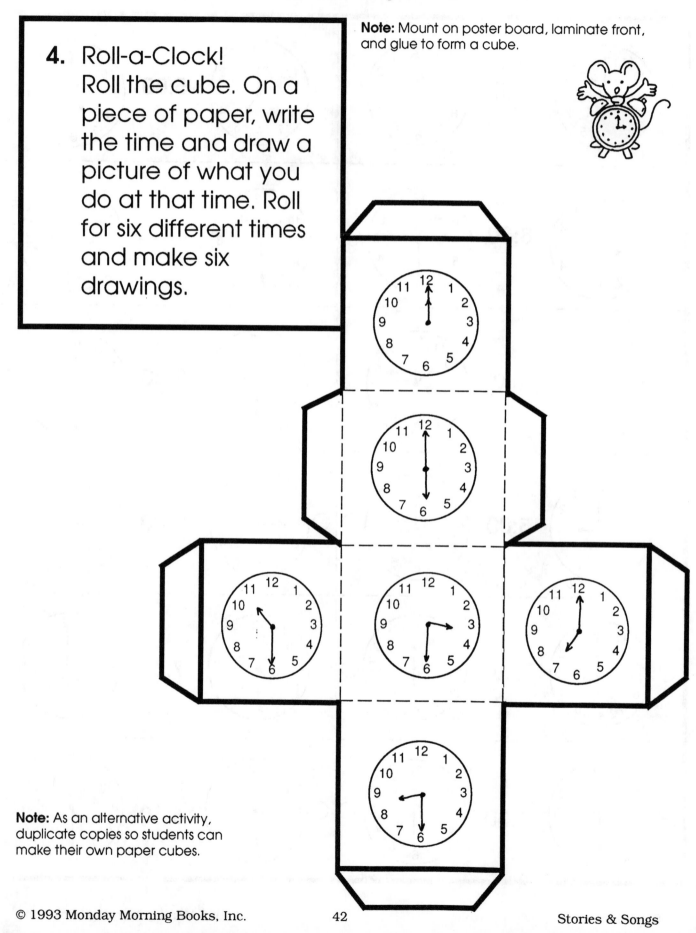

Note: As an alternative activity, duplicate copies so students can make their own paper cubes.

Hickory Dickory Dock

5. Draw in the missing clock hand on each card to show the right time.

Note: Duplicate clock cards and store in pocket on center.

Maria comes at 2:00.	Shelly comes at 9:30.
Roger comes at 3:30.	Lee comes at 12:30.
Jose comes at 11:00.	Susan comes at 5:00.

Hickory Dickory Dock

Glenda comes at 1:30.

Tomas comes at 3:00.

Rosa comes at 4:00.

Cristen comes at 7:30.

Paul comes at 10:30.

Greg comes at 8:00.

Jamie comes at 9:00.

Juan comes at 2:30.

Tim comes at 5:30.

Jamal comes at 6:00.

Sing a Song of Sixpence

Materials:
Storage pockets, two-inch brad, tape,
poster board, glue, rubber stamp coin set,
student paper, magnetic tape, paper clips.

Money to 25¢

46

Sing a Song of Sixpence

Sing a Song of Sixpence

Sing a Song of Sixpence

1. Take the cards from the pocket. Match the pictures with the correct coins. Flip over to check.

Note: Color-code backs of cards for self-checking. Store in pocket on center.

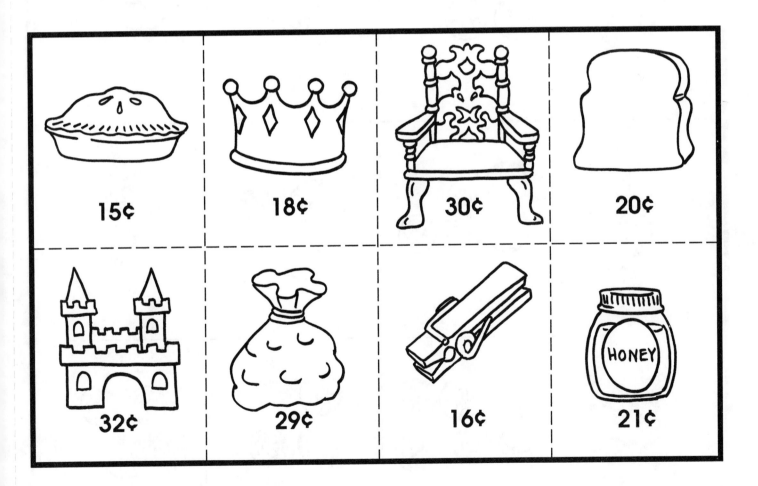

15¢   18¢   30¢   20¢

32¢   29¢   16¢   21¢

Sing a Song of Sixpence

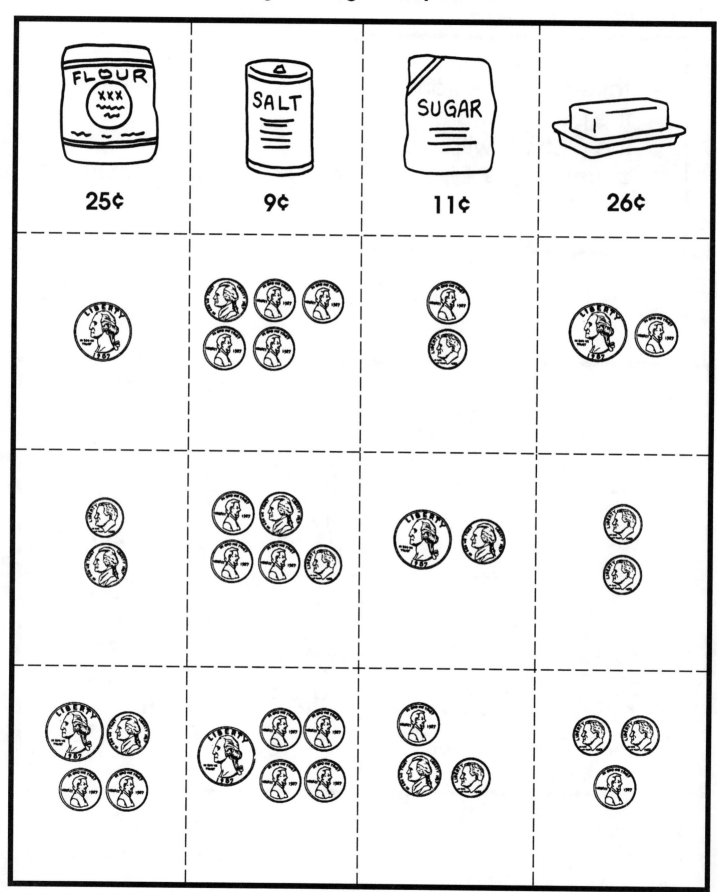

Sing a Song of Sixpence

2. Number a piece of paper from 1 to 8. Spin the dial. List the coins you need. Continue to spin. If you spin the same amount twice, write a different coin combination. Check your work with the answer key.

Note: If you have a coin stamp set, you may want students to stamp out the coins they need for this activity.

Answer Key

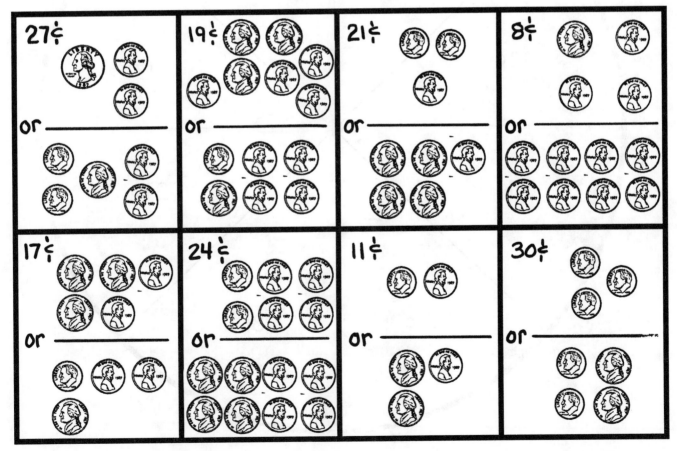

Note: Store folded in pocket on center.

Sing a Song of Sixpence

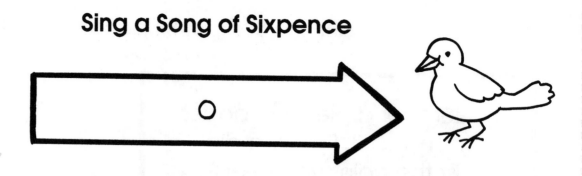

Note: Mount arrow on poster board and attach to wheel and center with a two-inch brad.

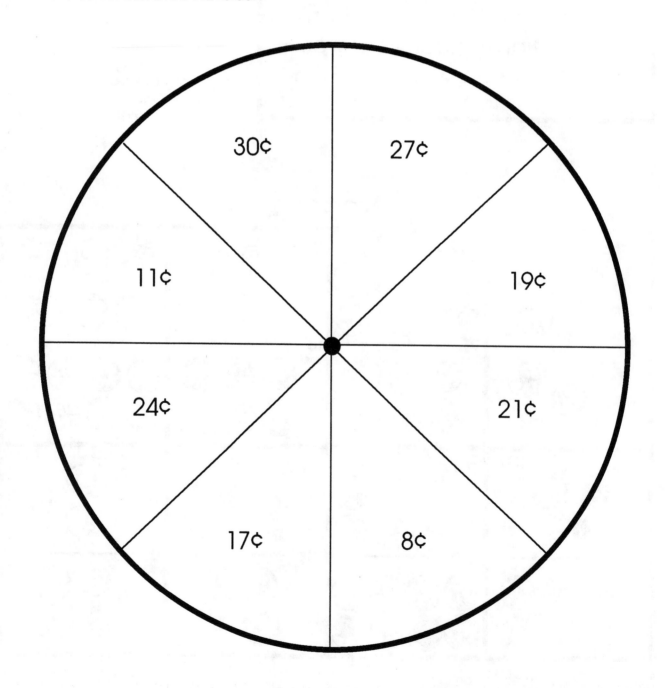

Sing a Song of Sixpence

3. Count the coins in the money bags. Write the amounts on your paper.

4. The King has one quarter to spend. How much money will he get back from each purchase on the shopping list? Press a coin card on the tape to make the correct change.

Note: Cut out cards and attach a paper clip to each. Store in pocket on center.

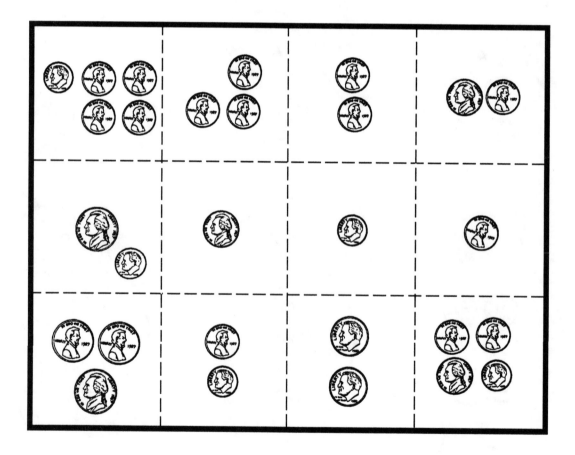

Sing a Song of Sixpence

Note: Place squares of magnetic tape where indicated .

Royal Shopping List

23¢

10¢

8¢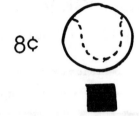

15¢

18¢

14¢

20¢

5¢

11¢

24¢

22¢

19¢

Sing a Song of Sixpence

5. Take a coin strip from the pocket. Fill in the blanks. Check your answers with the answer key.

Note: Duplicate coin strip and store in pocket on center, along with the answer key.

Coin Strip					Answer Key				
	quarter	dime	nickel	penny		quarter	dime	nickel	penny
17¢	0	1	1	__	17¢	0	1	1	2
26¢	__	0	0	1	26¢	1	0	0	1
32¢	0	2	__	2	32¢	0	2	2	2
11¢	0	0	__	1	11¢	0	0	2	1
28¢	1	0	0	__	28¢	1	0	0	3
21¢	0	__	0	1	21¢	0	2	0	1
13¢	0	0	__	3	13¢	0	0	2	3
18¢	0	1	__	3	18¢	0	1	1	3
20¢	0	1	__	0	20¢	0	1	2	0
12¢	0	0	__	2	12¢	0	0	2	2

The Gingerbread Man

Materials:
Storage pockets, three paper cups,
scissors, crayons, glue, poster board,
hole punch, string, two-inch brad,
student paper.

The Gingerbread Man

1.

$\frac{4}{4}$ $\frac{1}{2}$ $\frac{4}{5}$ $\frac{2}{3}$ $\frac{1}{4}$ $\frac{3}{5}$ $\frac{1}{5}$ $\frac{2}{3}$ $\frac{2}{2}$ $\frac{3}{4}$ $\frac{1}{3}$

FLOUR

SUGAR

2.

3.

4.

5.

COOKIE SHEETS

$\frac{2}{3}$ $\frac{3}{4}$ $\frac{4}{5}$

$\frac{1}{2}$ $\frac{1}{2}$ $\frac{1}{5}$ $\frac{1}{3}$ $\frac{1}{3}$ $\frac{2}{3}$ $\frac{1}{3}$ $\frac{1}{2}$

Create-a-Cookie!

Fractions

The Gingerbread Man

The Gingerbread Man

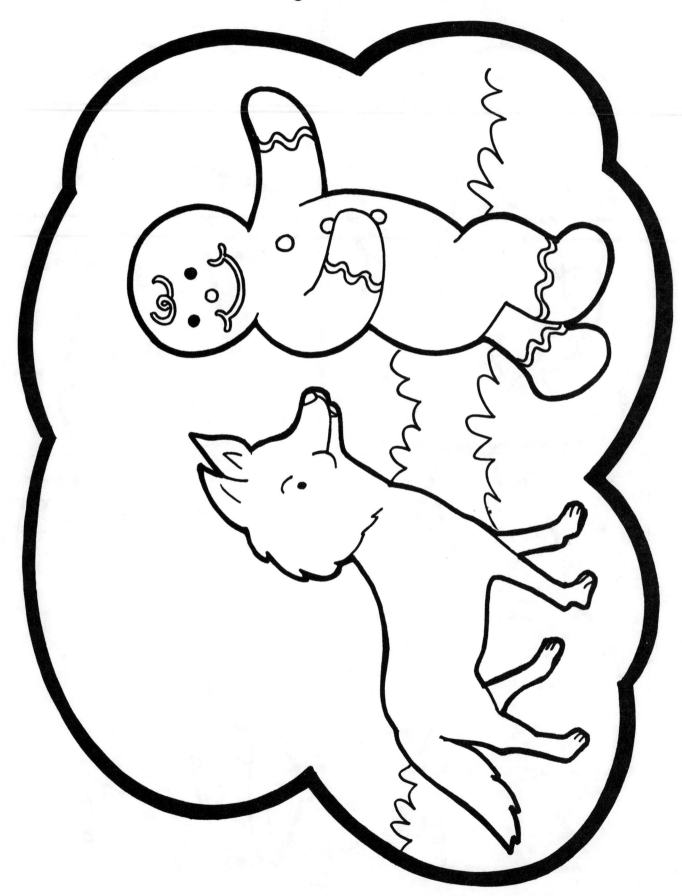

The Gingerbread Man

The Gingerbread Man

1. Spin a fraction. Take a card from the pocket. Cut out the right number of boxes for the bigger part of the fraction. Color in the right number of boxes for the smaller part of the fraction. Glue the fraction picture on your paper and label it. Spin to make 10 different fraction pictures.

Note: Have several sample fraction pictures displayed at center. Duplicate multiple copies of fraction blanks below and store in pocket on center.

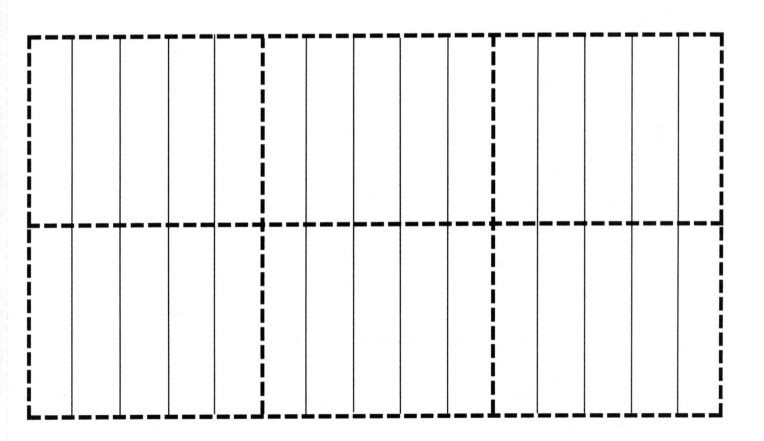

The Gingerbread Man

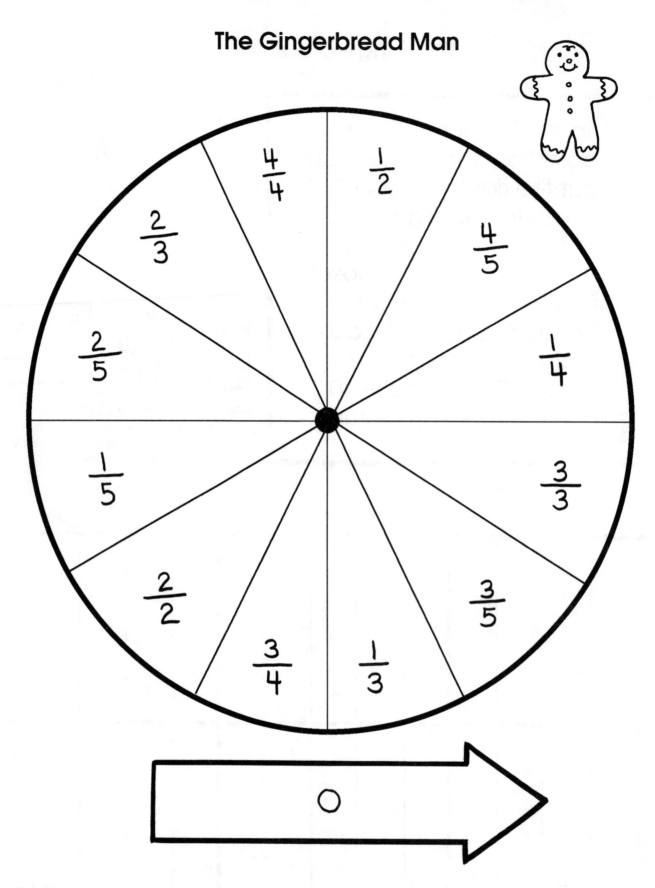

Note: Mount arrow on poster board and attach to wheel and center with two-inch brad.

         Stories & Songs

The Gingerbread Man

2. Take the picture cards from the pocket. Put the correct cards in each cup. Flip the cards over to check.

Note: Label paper cups as follows: 2/3, 3/4, 4/5. Code the backs of the picture cards and store in pocket on center.

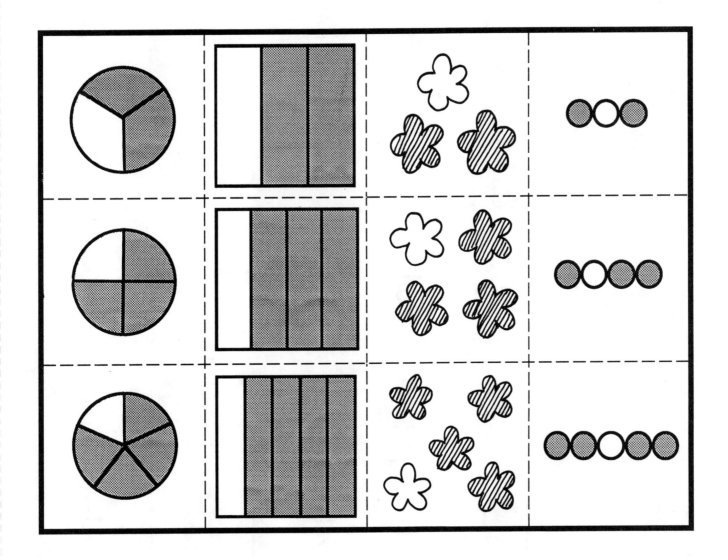

The Gingerbread Man

3. On each card, punch a hole beside the fraction that matches the picture.

Note: Use a string to tie your hole punch to the center. Store punch cards in pocket on center.

○ $\frac{1}{4}$ ⬡ (circle) $\frac{1}{3}$○○ $\frac{3}{4}$ ⬜ (square) $\frac{3}{1}$○

○ $\frac{5}{3}$ ▦ (bars) $\frac{3}{5}$○○ $\frac{1}{2}$ ❀ (flowers) $\frac{1}{3}$○

○ $\frac{1}{4}$ ❀ (flowers) $\frac{1}{3}$○○ $\frac{3}{5}$ ●●○○● (circles) $\frac{2}{3}$○

○ $\frac{2}{3}$ ○●● (circles) $\frac{2}{2}$○○ $\frac{1}{4}$ ⬟ (circle fifths) $\frac{1}{5}$○

○ $\frac{1}{4}$ ⬤ (circle) $\frac{4}{4}$○○ $\frac{1}{3}$ ▥ (bars) $\frac{1}{2}$○

The Gingerbread Man

Note: Store cards in pocket on center.

4. Concentration Game for Two Players

1. Shuffle the cards and place them face down.

2. In turn, try to turn over a matching fraction and picture.

3. If you get a match, keep the cards. If you do not get a match, turn the cards back down.

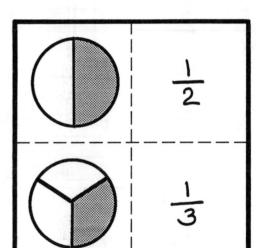

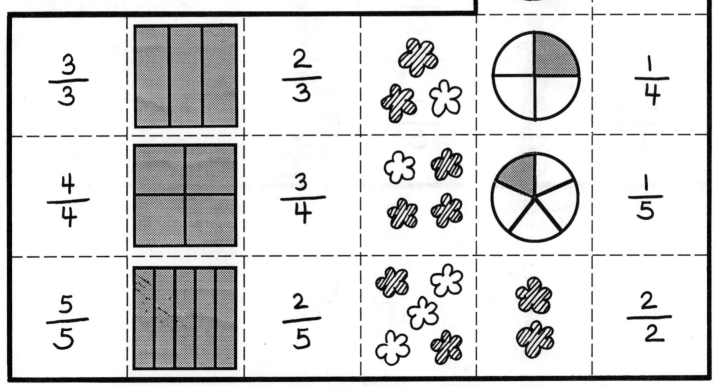

The Gingerbread Man

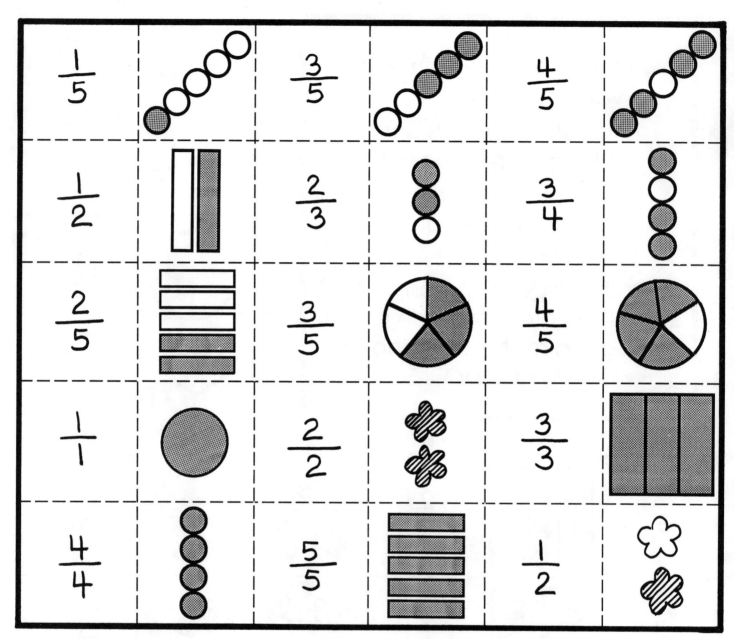

Note: As students become proficient with activity, increase number of cards.

Stories & Songs

The Gingerbread Man

5. Create-a-Cookie

Each player needs a cookie sheet card and a crayon.

1. In turn, pick a picture card and give the fraction. Check the answer key.

2. For each correct answer, draw in one of these on the gingerbread cookie.

-right eye   -cap

-left eye   -right mitten

-nose   -left mitten

-mouth   -right boot

-bow tie   -left boot

Answer Key	
1. 1/3	16. 1/2
2. 3/4	17. 3/3
3. 1/5	18. 5/5
4. 3/4	19. 2/2
5. 2/3	20. 2/5
6. 2/2	21. 2/2
7. 2/5	22. 2/3
8. 1/2	23. 1/5
9. 1/3	24. 3/5
10 1/4	25. 2/3
11. 1/3	26. 4/5
12. 3/5	27. 4/5
13. 3/3	28. 1/2
14. 3/4	29. 1/4
15. 1/4	

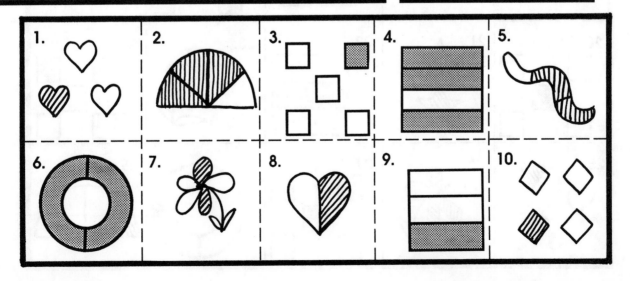

The Gingerbread Man

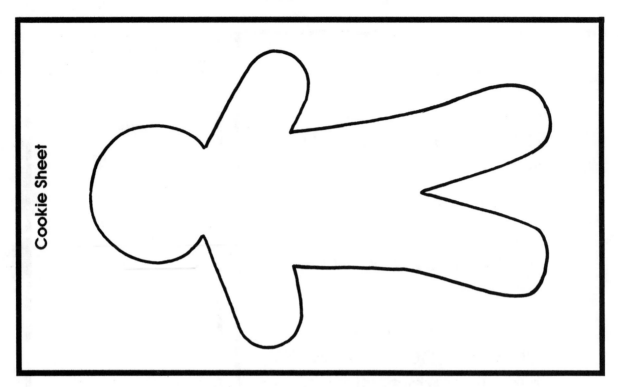

Cookie Sheet

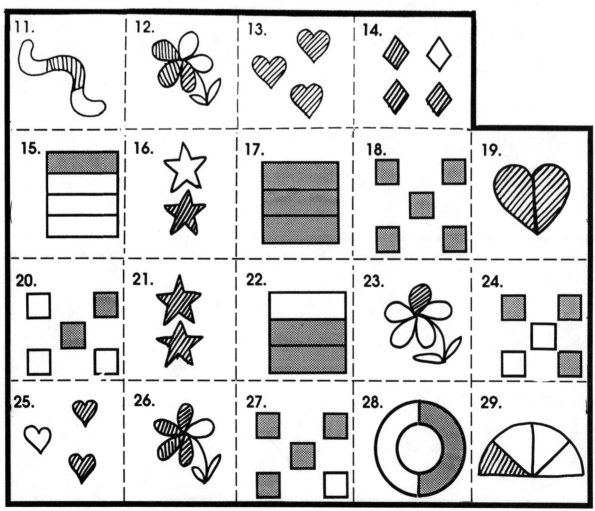

Jack and the Beanstalk

Jack
and the
Beanstalk

1.

2.

3.

4.

5.

Meter or Centimeter?
a crayon
a football field
a truck
a dollar bill
a playground slide
a safety pin
a cookie
a garden hose
a banana
a road
a ladder
a Ping-Pong ball

Measurement

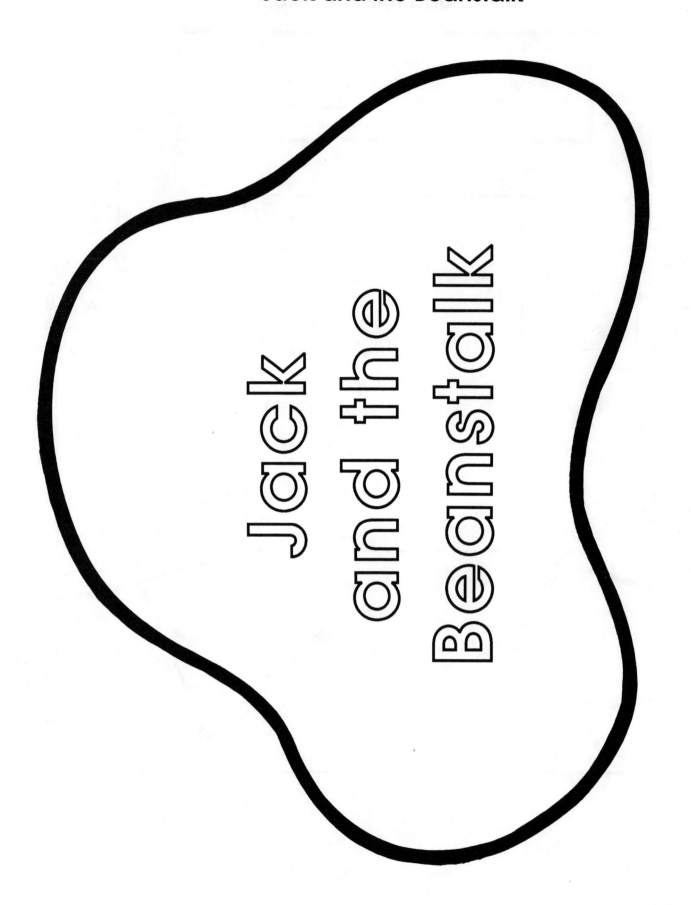

Jack and the Beanstalk

Jack and the Beanstalk

Jack and the Beanstalk

1. Use a centimeter ruler to measure these things. Write the answers on the measurement sheet.

   1. a pencil   6. a friend's nose

   2. a paper clip   7. a toy car

   3. your little finger   8. a piece of string

   4. your foot   9. a dime

   5. an eraser   10. a book

Jack and the Beanstalk

2. Use a meter stick to measure these things. Write the answers on the measurement sheet.

1. a blackboard

2. a table

3. a friend

4. a window

5. a teacher

6. the width of a hall

7. the length of a wall

8. a door

9. a length of rope

10. a line of kids

Jack and the Beanstalk

Note: Place items to be measured at learning center along with centimeter rulers and meter sticks. Duplicate answer sheets below and store in appropriate pockets. A blank sheet is provided so children may choose other items to measure.

Centimeter Measurement Sheet	Meter Measurement Sheet	Your choice! Pick 10 things to measure.
1. a pencil = _____	1. a blackboard = _____	1. _____ = _____
2. a paper clip = _____	2. a table = _____	2. _____ = _____
3. your little finger = _____	3. a friend = _____	3. _____ = _____
4. your foot = _____	4. a window = _____	4. _____ = _____
5. an eraser = _____	5. a teacher = _____	5. _____ = _____
6. a friend's nose = _____	6. the width of a hall = _____	6. _____ = _____
7. a toy car = _____	7. the length of a wall = ___	7. _____ = _____
8. a piece of string = _____	8. a door = _____	8. _____ = _____
9. a dime = _____	9. a length of tape = _____	9. _____ = _____
10. a book = _____	10. a line of kids = _____	10. _____ = _____

Jack and the Beanstalk

3. Punch the best unit of measurement for each thing on the problem sheet.

Note: Use string to tie hole punch to learning center. The activity may also be completed by coloring in the correct circles. Duplicate punch strips and store in pocket on center.

○ Meter or Centimeter? ○	○ Meter or Centimeter? ○
○ a giant ○	○ a crayon ○
○ tiny magic beans ○	○ a football field ○
○ a beanstalk ○	○ a truck ○
○ a castle ○	○ a dollar bill ○
○ Jack ○	○ a playground slide ○
○ an ant ○	○ a safety pin ○
○ an egg ○	○ a cookie ○
○ a cow ○	○ a garden hose ○
○ a giant's bed ○	○ a banana ○
○ a hen ○	○ a road ○
○ a cloud ○	○ a ladder ○
○ a gold coin ○	○ a Ping-Pong ball ○

Jack and the Beanstalk

4. Silly Centimeters

Pick any eight cards. Use a centimeter ruler to draw the pictures on your paper.

Note: Store cards in pocket on center. Provide crayons, paper, and centimeter rulers.

Draw a snake 15 cm. long.	Draw a flower 5 cm. high.	Draw a tree 12 cm. tall.	Draw a mouse with a 2 cm. tail.
Draw a house 7 cm. high.	Draw a cat 10 cm. high.	Draw a giant 16 cm. tall.	Draw a magic bean 1 cm. long.

Jack and the Beanstalk

Draw a beanstalk 9 cm. high.	Draw a boy 6 cm. tall.	Draw a lake 8 cm. long.
Draw a castle 18 cm. high.	Draw a treasure chest 4 cm. long.	Draw a harp 6 cm. tall.
Draw a kite with a 4 cm. tail.	Draw an airplane with wings 5 cm. long.	Draw an ax with a 3 cm. handle.
Draw a turtle with a shell 3 cm. long.	Draw a giant footprint 7 cm. long.	Draw a mountain 20 cm. high.

Stories & Songs

Jack and the Beanstalk

5. Magic Bean Construction Company

Test your metric building skills! Pick a card and follow the directions.

Note: Provide meter sticks and building materials as indicated. Store direction cards in pocket on center.

Tape together sheets of old newspaper to measure 4 meters long. Draw a 3 meter beanstalk. Make Jack 1 meter tall.

Stack up books to measure 3 meters high. Place paper leaves 1 meter apart up the stack.

Jack and the Beanstalk

Use chalk to draw a 5 meter beanstalk on pavement. Draw a castle at the top that is 2 meters tall.

With masking tape, make a line in the hall that is 4 meters long. Place a star at the 2 meter mark.

Collect cardboard boxes to build a train that is 3 meters long. Make a cardboard passenger that is two meters tall.

Stretch out a rope that is 6 meters long. Mark each meter on the rope with a permanent marker.

 Stories & Songs

Old MacDonald

Materials:
Storage pockets, paper cup,
clothespin, two two-inch brads,
magnetic tape, paper clips,
hole punch, poster board, glue, string.

Subtraction

82

Old MacDonald

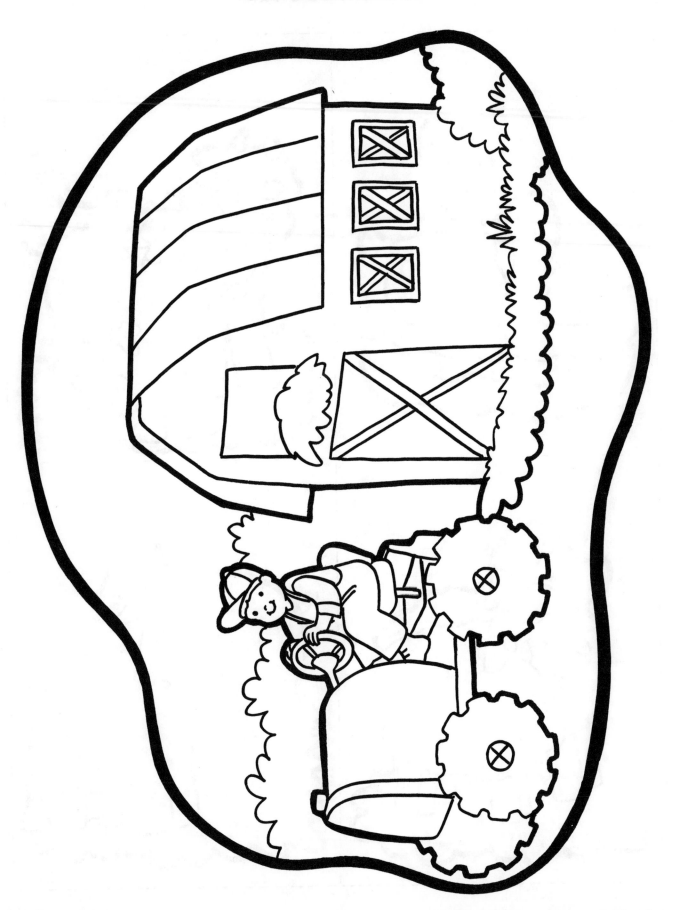

© 1993 Monday Morning Books, Inc.

Old MacDonald

84   *Stories & Songs*

Old MacDonald

1. Turn the arrow on each wheel. Press a number card on the tape after the equal sign to make a true fact.

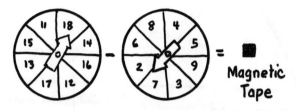

Magnetic Tape

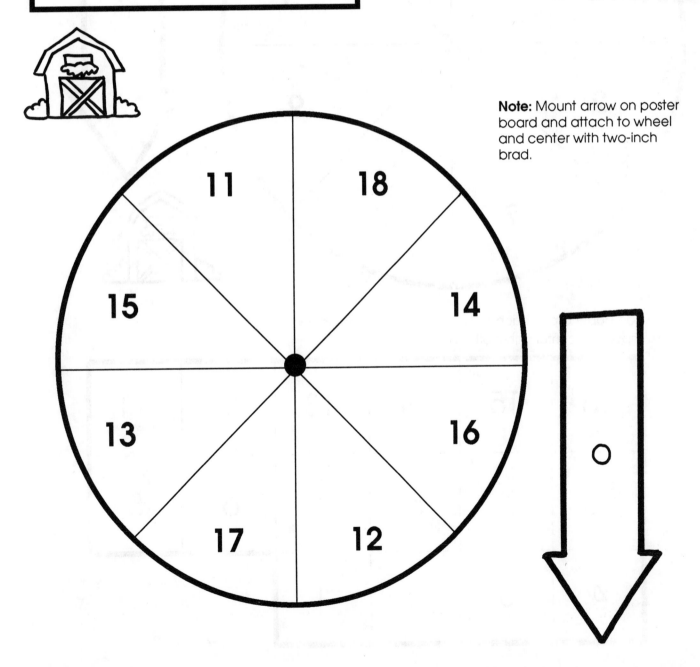

Old MacDonald

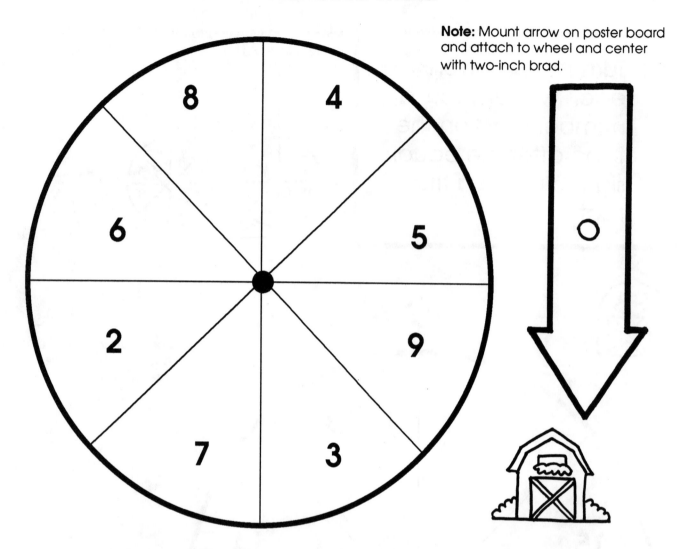

Note: Mount arrow on poster board and attach to wheel and center with two-inch brad.

Add paper clip to each number card. Store cards in cup clipped to center with clothespin.

16	15	14	13	12	11
10	9	8	7	6	5
4	3	2	1		

Stories & Songs

Old MacDonald

Note: Store cards in pocket on center. If desired, code backs "I" or "C" for self-checking.

2. Find the correct facts. Did you find 12 of them?

$15 - 8 = 7$	$15 - 6 = 8$	$11 - 4 = 7$
$14 - 7 = 7$	$18 - 9 = 9$	$12 - 5 = 7$
$17 - 13 = 4$	$12 - 8 = 5$	$18 - 6 = 12$
$17 - 9 = 7$	$16 - 10 = 6$	$18 - 9 = 8$
$13 - 7 = 8$	$14 - 8 = 6$	$15 - 9 = 6$
$16 - 9 = 7$	$11 - 3 = 7$	$13 - 9 = 4$

Old MacDonald

3. Punch the correct answer for each problem on the problem sheet.

Note: Use a string to tie hole punch to center. Duplicate punch strips and store in pocket.

The activity may also be completed by coloring in the correct circles.

$11 - 6 =$	5 ⭕ 6 ⭕	$10 - 7 =$	3 ⭕ 4 ⭕
$17 - 9 =$	6 ⭕ 8 ⭕	$13 - 6 =$	9 ⭕ 7 ⭕
$14 - 6 =$	7 ⭕ 8 ⭕	$17 - 5 =$	12 ⭕ 11 ⭕
$18 - 9 =$	9 ⭕ 11 ⭕	$12 - 8 =$	6 ⭕ 4 ⭕
$15 - 8 =$	9 ⭕ 7 ⭕	$15 - 9 =$	8 ⭕ 6 ⭕
$10 - 4 =$	6 ⭕ 7 ⭕	$18 - 10 =$	8 ⭕ 11 ⭕
$13 - 4 =$	8 ⭕ 9 ⭕	$15 - 6 =$	11 ⭕ 9 ⭕
$16 - 7 =$	9 ⭕ 8 ⭕	$14 - 5 =$	9 ⭕ 8 ⭕
$12 - 9 =$	4 ⭕ 3 ⭕	$11 - 3 =$	9 ⭕ 8 ⭕
$14 - 7 =$	7 ⭕ 6 ⭕	$16 - 8 =$	10 ⭕ 8 ⭕

Stories & Songs

Old MacDonald

4. Barnyard Code
Use the picture code to solve each problem on the problem sheet. Draw the picture for the correct answer.

Picture Code

4 = (doghouse)   9 = (boot)   14 = (circle)

5 = (cat)   10 = (tulip)   15 = (moon)

6 = (hat)   11 = (shirt)   16 = (star)

7 = (rectangle)   12 = (bow tie)   17 = (heart)

8 = (duck)   13 = (cup)   18 = (flower)

Old MacDonald

Note: Duplicate problem sheet and store in pocket on center.

Old MacDonald

5. Go Fish Game for Two Players

1. Shuffle the problem cards.

2. Deal six cards to each player. Place the rest face down in a pile.

3. Look at your subtraction facts. If you have four cards that have the same remainder, discard them.

4. In turn, ask for cards with certain remainders from your partner. Draw from the pile if needed. Each time you have four cards with the same remainder, discard them.

5. The first to discard all fact cards wins!

Note: Store cards in pocket on center.

11 – 4	15 – 8	13 – 5
16 – 8	14 – 6	17 – 8
	18 – 9	

Old MacDonald

11 – 3	15 – 6	13 – 4
11 – 7	14 – 9	16 – 9
10 – 6	12 – 7	14 – 7
12 – 9	13 – 8	13 – 7
11 – 8	10 – 5	10 – 4
13 – 10	13 – 9	12 – 6
10 – 7	12 – 8	11 – 5

Tom Thumb

Materials:
Storage pockets, two paper cups, clothespins, hole punch, magnetic tape, paper clips, two two-inch brads, cup hooks, masking tape, poster board, glue, two different-colored sets of 12 checkers, student paper.

Greater Than, Less Than

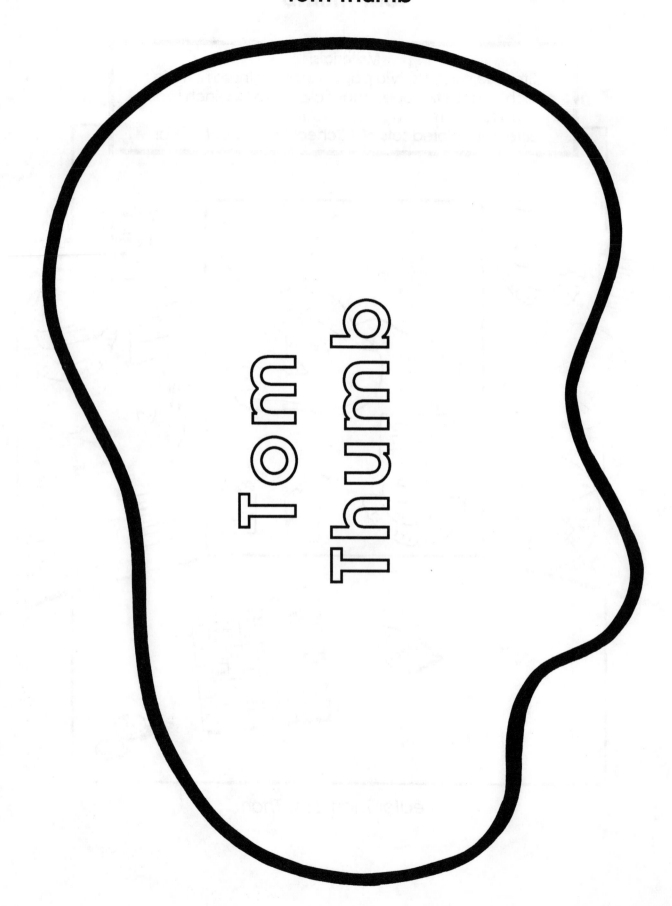

94

Tom Thumb

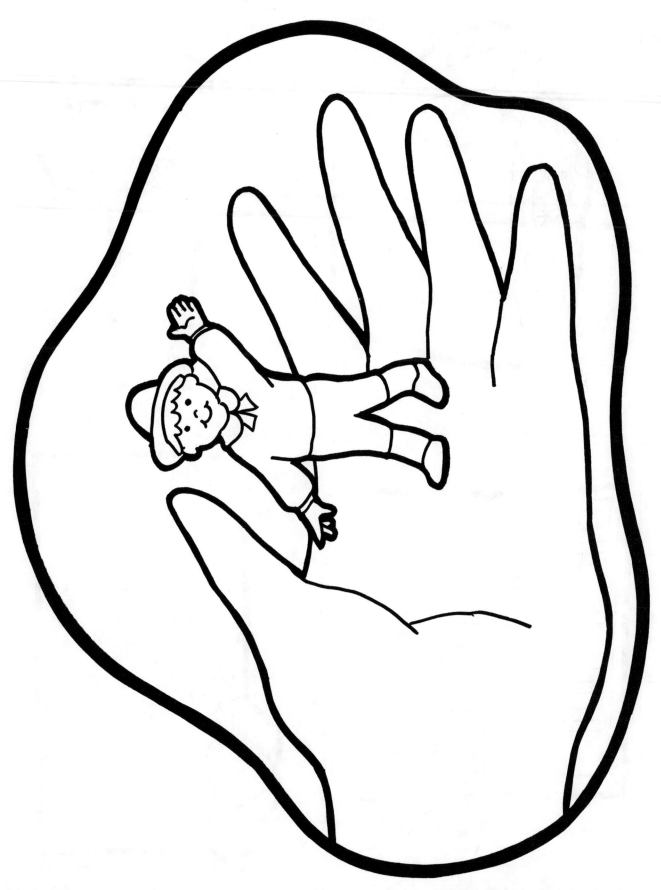

Tom Thumb

96

Tom Thumb

1. For Two Players

   1. In turn, pick a number card. Press it on the tape on either side of the wheel.

   2. Set the wheel to read < or >.

   3. Your partner must find a correct card to finish the number sentence.

Note: Slide a paper clip on each card. Store cards in pocket on center.

97	100	201	99	89	101
202	222	211	87	98	121
102	112	114	113	110	131
141	140	132	123	130	141

Tom Thumb

Note: Use two-inch brad to attach wheel to center.

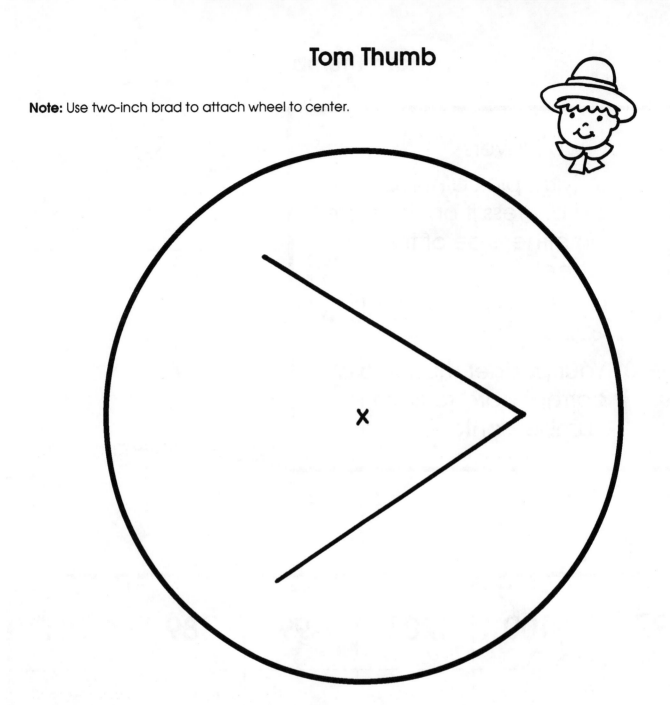

Mount a square of magnetic tape on both sides of wheel:

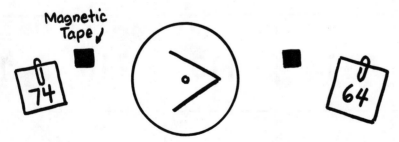

Students press number cards in place.

         Stories & Songs

Tom Thumb

2. Spin a number sentence. Write the sentence on your paper. Fill in the blank with a number from 1 to 999. Spin and write eight different number sentences.

Note: Use with number sentence wheel that follows.

3. Hang each tag on the right hook.

Note: See page 101 for tags. To attach metal cup hooks to center, poke a hole at each hook location. Thread the hook through the center from behind and secure the back with masking tape.

Tom Thumb

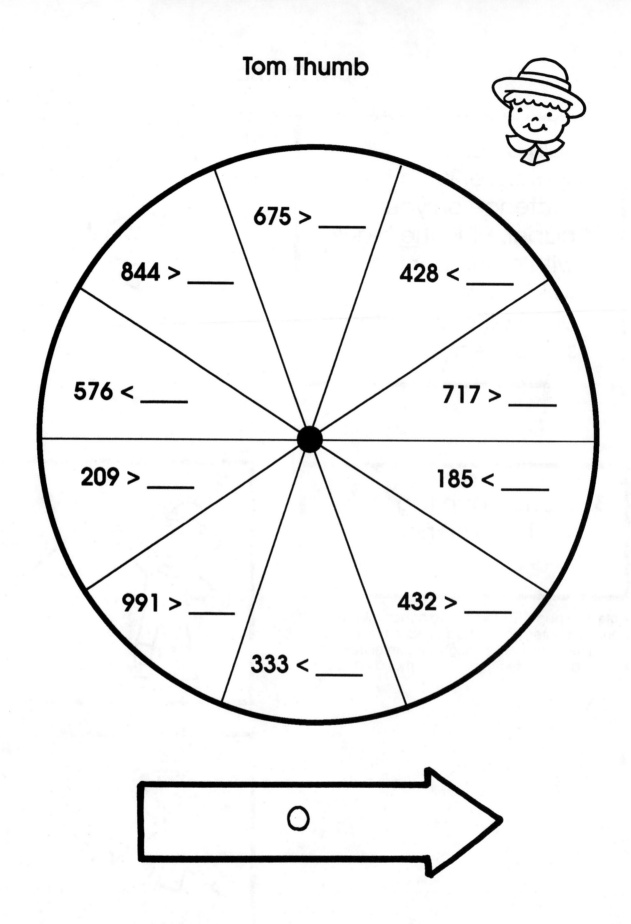

675 > ___

844 > ___

428 < ___

576 < ___

717 > ___

209 > ___

185 < ___

991 > ___

432 > ___

333 < ___

Note: Mount arrow on poster board and attach to wheel and center with two-inch brad.

100 Stories & Songs

Tom Thumb

Note: Punch holes in tags as indicated. Store tags in pocket on center.

◯	◯	◯
187 ___ 178	222 ___ 211	845 ___ 935
◯	◯	◯
601 ___ 106	863 ___ 763	699 ___ 701
◯	◯	◯
443 ___ 434	149 ___ 137	347 ___ 436
◯	◯	◯
528 ___ 527	901 ___ 910	782 ___ 877
◯	◯	◯
365 ___ 356	253 ___ 255	514 ___ 524

Tom Thumb

4. Put the correct facts in the cup marked "Thumbs Up!" Put the incorrect facts in the cup marked "Thumbs Down!"

Note: Clip paper cups to center with clothespins. Store fact cards in pocket.

Labels for paper cups:

 **Thumbs Up!**

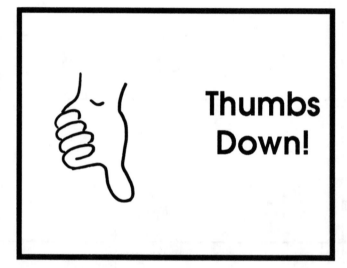 **Thumbs Down!**

775 > 770	452 < 451	108 < 110
313 > 331	864 > 846	291 > 289

Tom Thumb

536 < 538	**949 > 941**	**247 > 250**
87 < 102	**75 > 110**	**610 < 601**
511 < 521	**777 > 807**	**309 < 312**
180 < 201	**637 > 673**	**429 < 399**

5. Checkers Game for Two Players

1. Take the game board out of the pocket. Place your checkers on it.
2. Take turns moving from square to square.
3. To keep your square, tell if the number is > or < 597.

Note: To update the activity, put a square of magnetic tape over the number on the direction card. Press a new number card onto the magnetic square.

341

Tom Thumb

Note: Laminate and store folded in pocket on center.
Provide 12 checkers for each player.

657		583		491		777	
	353		810		600		549
426		799		318		596	
	635		291		904		443
594		875		497		962	
	212		698		346		587
730		828		464		998	
	392		555		747		275

 Stories & Songs

Pop Goes the Weasel

Materials:
Storage pockets, three paper cups, clothespins,
poster board, glue, three kinds of counters,
two-inch brad, wipe-off crayon, student paper.

Addition and Subtraction

Stories & Songs

Pop Goes the Weasel

107

Pop Goes the Weasel

108

Pop Goes the Weasel

1. Spin a number and use it to complete the problem below on your paper. Work the problem. Repeat until you have ten different problems.

```
  3 6
+
─────
```

```
  5 7
+
─────
```

```
  4 9
+
─────
```

```
  6 6
+
─────
```

Note: Post a different problem card each day.

Pop Goes the Weasel

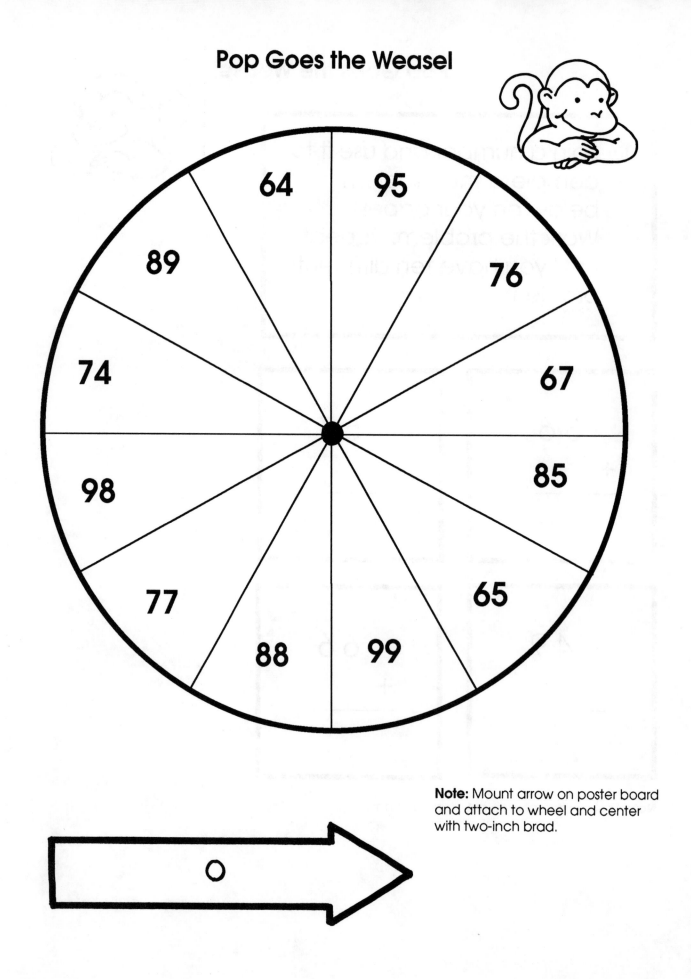

Note: Mount arrow on poster board and attach to wheel and center with two-inch brad.

Pop Goes the Weasel

2. Find the problem cards that have a difference of 16. Unscramble the code letters on those cards to find out what a cobbler does.

Note: Store cards in pocket on center. Correct problem cards, when unscrambled, will spell out "MENDS SHOES."

112 − 96 _____ **S**	223 −197 _____ **A**	303 −287 _____ **D**
215 −199 _____ **N**	104 − 88 _____ **E**	515 −488 _____ **T**

Pop Goes the Weasel

```
  402          384          112
 -386         -368         - 87
 ─────        ─────        ─────

    M            S            F
```

```
  114          163          505
 - 88         -147         -489
 ─────        ─────        ─────

    U            H            O
```

```
  492          403          213
 -476         -386         -197
 ─────        ─────        ─────

    E            W            S
```

112   Stories & Songs

Pop Goes the Weasel

3. Take a problem sheet from the pocket. Use a wipe-off crayon to color in the circle beside each correct problem.

Note: Laminate the problem sheets. Store in pocket on center and provide a wipe-off crayon.

167 + 35 —— 202 ○	83 + 28 —— 111 ○	97 + 48 —— 146 ○
162 + 58 —— 220 ○	136 + 77 —— 213 ○	109 + 92 —— 201 ○
198 + 84 —— 282 ○	179 + 63 —— 252 ○	78 + 58 —— 137 ○
155 + 56 —— 211 ○	57 + 68 —— 125 ○	99 + 33 —— 221 ○

Pop Goes the Weasel

423 −279 —— 144 ○	202 − 77 —— 135 ○	230 − 97 —— 143 ○
385 − 97 —— 288 ○	464 −188 —— 266 ○	321 − 82 —— 229 ○
352 − 87 —— 265 ○	321 −178 —— 143 ○	232 − 36 —— 196 ○
258 − 79 —— 177 ○	336 − 69 —— 259 ○	243 − 56 —— 187 ○

4. For Two Students

Each student takes a problem card. Use the place value counters to explain your problem to your partner.

Note: Provide three kinds of counters (ones, tens, hundreds) and store in paper cups clipped with clothespins to the center.

 Stories & Songs

Pop Goes the Weasel

Ones	Tens	Hundreds

$$
\begin{array}{r}
214 \\
-\ 77 \\
\hline
137
\end{array}
\qquad
\begin{array}{r}
163 \\
+\ 79 \\
\hline
242
\end{array}
\qquad
\begin{array}{r}
256 \\
-\ 98 \\
\hline
158
\end{array}
\qquad
\begin{array}{r}
228 \\
-\ 89 \\
\hline
139
\end{array}
$$

$$
\begin{array}{r}
135 \\
+\ 67 \\
\hline
202
\end{array}
\qquad
\begin{array}{r}
36 \\
+\ 74 \\
\hline
110
\end{array}
\qquad
\begin{array}{r}
146 \\
+\ 95 \\
\hline
241
\end{array}
$$

Note: Store problem cards in pocket on center.

5. Concentration Game for Two Players

   1. Shuffle the problem and answer cards and place them face down.

   2. In turn, try to turn over a matching problem and answer.

   3. If you make a match, keep the cards. If the cards do not match, turn them back down.

   4. Play until all cards are matched.

Pop Goes the Weasel

46 + 74	138 + 62	127 + 86	57 + 65
120	200	213	122
99 + 67	187 + 29	343 – 128	241 – 99
166	216	215	142
310 – 189	481 – 278	216 – 79	421 – 179
121	203	137	242

Note: Store cards in pocket on center.

Stories & Songs

I've Been Working on the Railroad

Materials:
Wipe-off crayons, game timers,
storage pockets, game markers,
2 colors of poster board, glue,
crayons, student paper.

I've Been Working on the Railroad

Crazy Caboose

Multiplication to 45

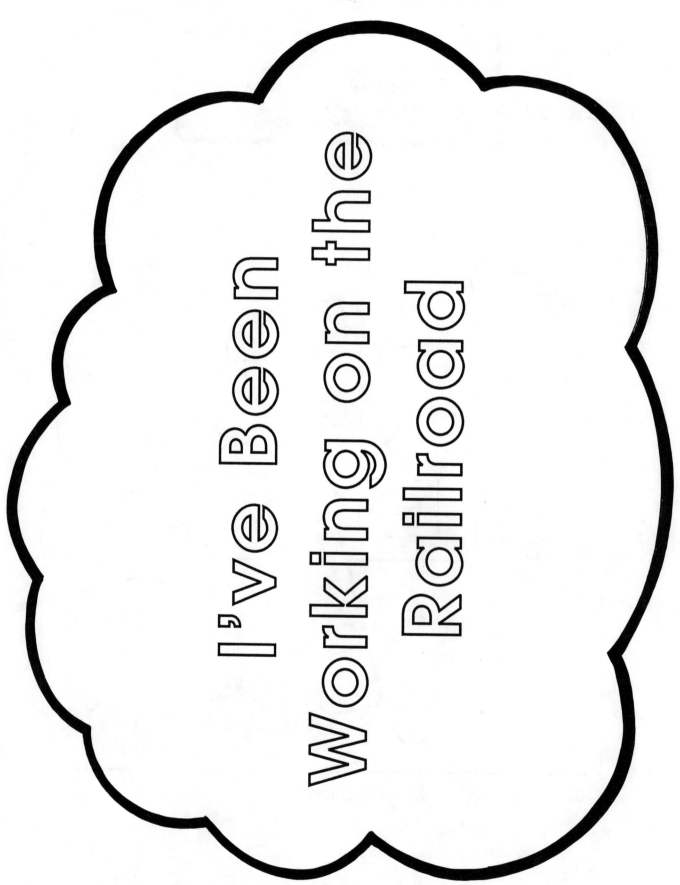

118

I've Been Working on the Railroad

I've Been Working on the Railroad

120

Stories & Songs

I've Been Working on the Railroad

1. Take a "Making Tracks" sheet from the pocket. Then choose five cards. Follow the directions.

Note: store direction cards in pocket on center. Provide the necessary colors of crayons.

Color red the problems that equal 12.	Color green the problems that equal 20.	Color purple the problems that equal 27.
Color yellow the problems that equal 9.	Color blue the problems that equal 15.	Color orange the problems that equal 24.
Color pink the problems that equal 18.	Color brown the problems that equal 36.	Color gray the problems that equal 21.

I've Been Working on the Railroad

Note: Duplicate and store in pocket on center.

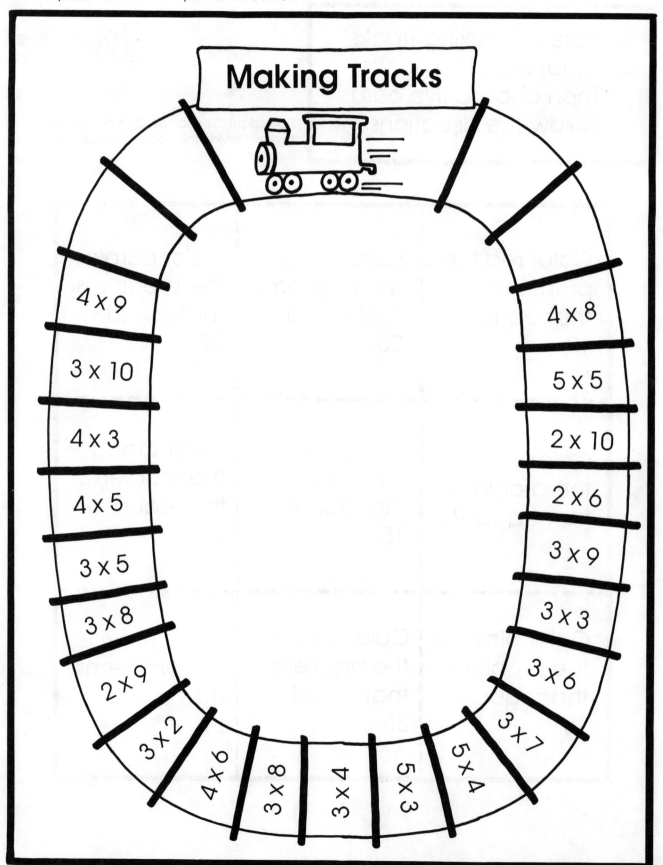

Making Tracks

4 x 9
3 x 10
4 x 3
4 x 5
3 x 5
3 x 8
2 x 9
3 x 2
4 x 6
3 x 8
3 x 4
5 x 3
5 x 4
3 x 7
3 x 6
3 x 3
3 x 9
2 x 6
2 x 10
5 x 5
4 x 8

I've Been Working on the Railroad

2. Put the engines on the table. Place each problem circle on the engine that shows the missing number. Flip problems over to check.

Note: Label backs of problem circles with missing factors for self-checking. Store with engines in pocket on center.

Missing Factor: 9

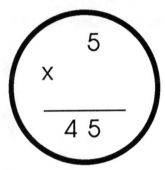

$$\begin{array}{r} 5 \\ \times \\ \hline 4\,5 \end{array}$$

$$\begin{array}{r} 4 \\ \times \\ \hline 3\,6 \end{array}$$

$$\begin{array}{r} 3 \\ \times \\ \hline 2\,7 \end{array}$$

$$\begin{array}{r} 2 \\ \times \\ \hline 1\,8 \end{array}$$

Missing Factor: 8

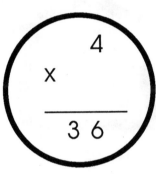
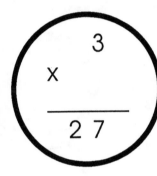
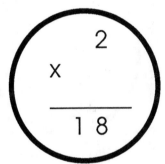

$$\begin{array}{r} 6 \\ \times \\ \hline 4\,8 \end{array}$$

$$\begin{array}{r} 5 \\ \times \\ \hline 4\,0 \end{array}$$

$$\begin{array}{r} 4 \\ \times \\ \hline 3\,2 \end{array}$$

$$\begin{array}{r} 3 \\ \times \\ \hline 2\,4 \end{array}$$

Missing Factor: 7

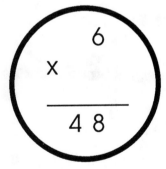
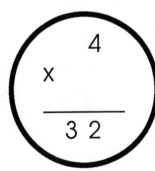
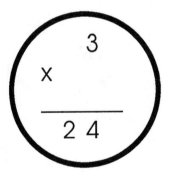
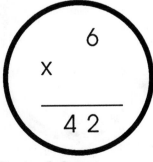
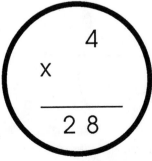
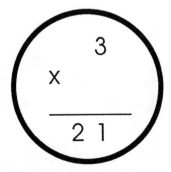

$$\begin{array}{r} 6 \\ \times \\ \hline 4\,2 \end{array}$$

$$\begin{array}{r} 5 \\ \times \\ \hline 3\,5 \end{array}$$

$$\begin{array}{r} 4 \\ \times \\ \hline 2\,8 \end{array}$$

$$\begin{array}{r} 3 \\ \times \\ \hline 2\,1 \end{array}$$

I've Been Working on the Railroad

Incorrect problem circles

6
x
___
4 5

6
x
___
2 1

3
x
___
2 2

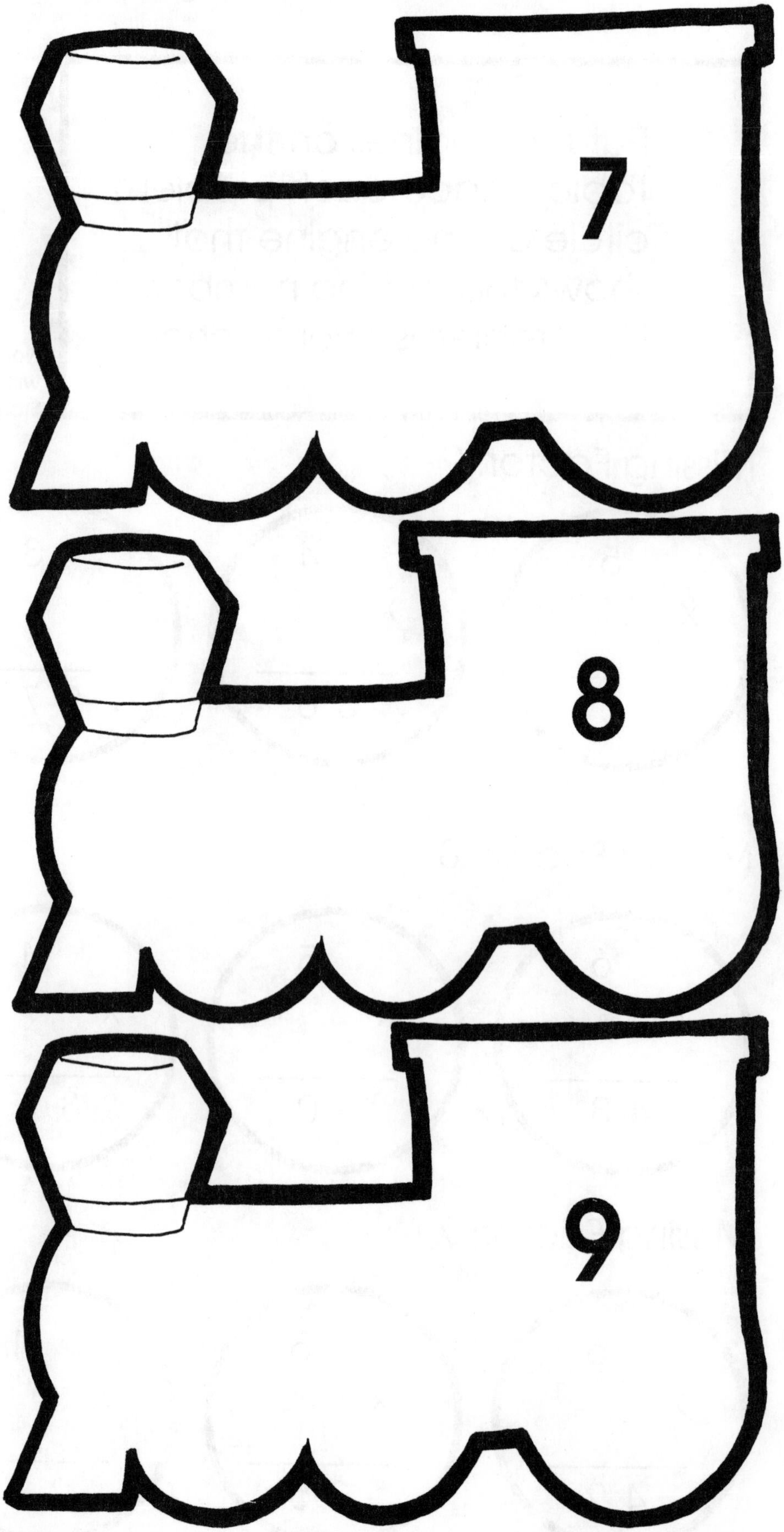

7

8

9

Stories & Songs

I've Been Working on the Railroad

3. For Two Students

   1. Put a number in each box on a drill strip.

   2. Give the strip to your partner to complete.

   3. Use a timer. Record your partner's time at the bottom of the strip.

Note: Provide a small game timer. Duplicate drill strips and store in pocket on center.

4 x ☐ = _____

8 x ☐ = _____

6 x ☐ = _____

9 x ☐ = _____

1 x ☐ = _____

5 x ☐ = _____

10 x ☐ = _____

2 x ☐ = _____

7 x ☐ = _____

3 x ☐ = _____

Time:_____

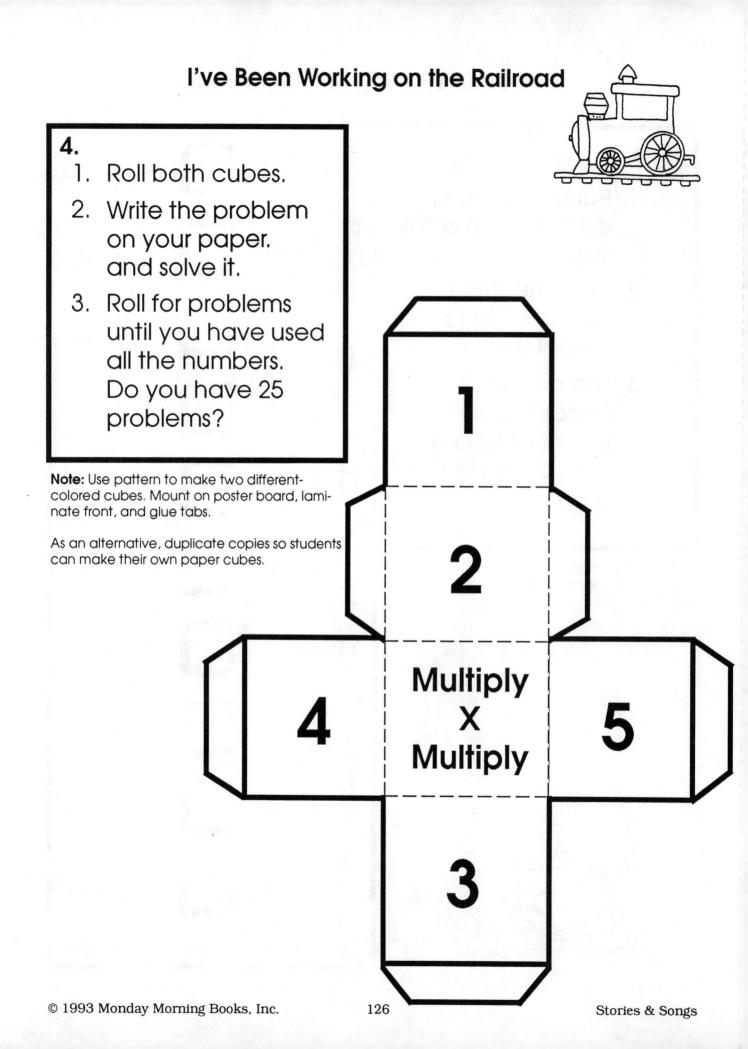

4.

1. Roll both cubes.

2. Write the problem on your paper. and solve it.

3. Roll for problems until you have used all the numbers. Do you have 25 problems?

Note: Use pattern to make two different-colored cubes. Mount on poster board, laminate front, and glue tabs.

As an alternative, duplicate copies so students can make their own paper cubes.

1

2

Multiply
x
Multiply

4

5

3

I've Been Working on the Railroad

5. Game for Two Players

1. Put the game board on the table.

2. Shuffle the problem cards and place one face up.

3. Decide if the problem is correct or incorrect. Flip the card over to check. If you are right, move ahead two spaces. If you are wrong, go back one space.

4. The first one to finish wins!

Note: Code backs of cards "I" or "C" for self-checking. Store with game board in pocket.

1.	2.	3.	4.	5.
5 X 9 = 45	4 X 5 = 20	5 X 3 = 16	3 X 3 = 9	4 X 6 = 25
6.	**7.**	**8.**	**9.**	**10.**
3 X 7 = 22	5 X 8 = 40	3 X 9 = 36	4 X 7 = 28	3 X 6 = 18
11.	**12.**	**13.**	**14.**	**15.**
3 X 8 = 24	4 X 3 = 18	5 X 7 = 32	4 X 9 = 27	5 X 4 = 20
16.	**17.**	**18.**	**19.**	**20.**
4 X 9 = 36	3 X 8 = 21	3 X 10 = 30	5 X 5 = 25	5 X 8 = 32
21.	**22.**	**23.**	**24.**	**25.**
3 X 4 = 12	3 X 5 = 20	5 X 6 = 30	3 X 6 = 24	4 X 8 = 32

I've Been Working on the Railroad

Note: Laminate game board and store folded in pocket on center. Provide game markers.

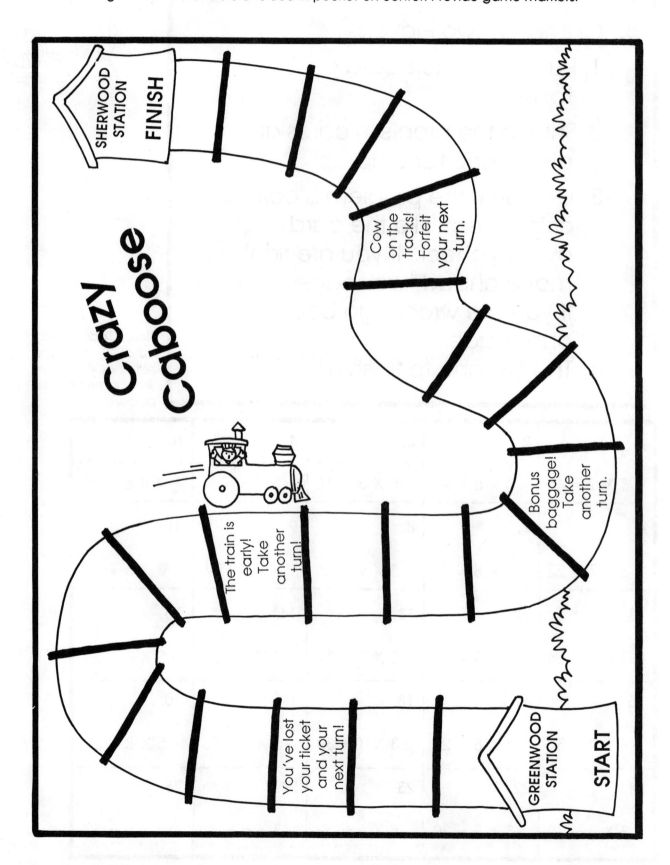